EXCEPT THE LORD
When God Became The Builder

Terika Smith, Ed.D.

Except The Lord Publishing

A Division of Terika Smith Ministries

Massachusetts

© 2015 by Dr. Terika T. Smith

A Division of Terika Smith Ministries

Massachusetts

© 2015 by Dr. Terika T. Smith

All rights reserved. No part of this book may be reproduced in any form without the permission in writing from the publisher, except in the case of brief quotations embodied in critical articles or reviews.

All scripture quotation unless otherwise indicted are taken from the New Living Translation Bible.

Book Design by Claudio Rafael

Manufactured in the United States of America
Printed in the United States of America

ISBN: 978-0-9965967-0-1
ISBN: 978-0-692-46569-1(ebook)

With Gratitude

This book is dedicated to the Loves of my life. There are so many people who fall into that category but especially I think of my parents, Bishop George and Rev. Evadney Smith. They have been a tremendous encouragement and inspiration in my life not because they are my parents but because of the consistency of their persona. They fear God above all. They are loving, giving, encouraging, relentless, persevering, and the list truly goes on. They are second to none; from the way they raised the four of us after migrating from Jamaica leaving everything to a country they did not know. The way they sacrificed at times working three jobs each while all six were in school at the same time. The way they challenged us, regardless our age to never quit, never give up, and always have a plan. My parents are dreamers and they inspire us to also be dreamers. It's not okay to just be, there is always more.

This book is dedicated to my siblings to include my in-laws: Marius and Karen Miclausi, Morvin and Diane Smith (Kurtis) and Dwight and Janis Smith. I am thankful to each of my siblings for their inspiration to want more, to never settling. Each of us has gleaned from the example of our parents and made conscious decisions to move forward. Each has our own families and profession yet we have the foundation that our parents taught us of Christ in the center and daring to be dreamers. We have all grown and gone in different directions yet we are anchored in the truth of our foundation. It is reassuring to know that regardless of where I am in this world, should I scrape a knee and my siblings learn of it, immediately my phone would be ringing or the doorbell. Thank you guys for being part of my inspiration. I am equally thankful for their spouses, my in-laws. Each has encouraged me to persevere; each has shown me support with the same love as though we were all from the same parents. Thank you

This book is dedicated to my nephews and niece: Omar Wisdom, Daniel Miclausi, Justin Smith, Jordan Smith, Sierra Smith, Dwight Smith Jr. From changing diapers to watching you now as adults, living your lives and in many ways following the same foundation established not by your parents but grandparents. The tenacity of mom and dad reflect the tenacity of grandma and granddaddy. I encourage you guys don't stop dreaming. Don't stop striving to do and be the best at what you do. I love you guys.

To my "mama" my "nutcracker" my "little lady", Karen Andujar. From the moment God gave me you to parent, I have loved you and felt even more inspired to become the best God has called me to be. I knew you were watching and I would tell the Lord, I wanted to be just like Him because you were watching. You were a HUGE inspiration for me in writing this book. I pray the transparency of this book serves as an inspiration for you to see that with God ALL things are possible. Your yesterday is behind you. God has a plan and you needed yesterday to be able to appreciate and step boldly into your destiny. I love you mama.

A special thank you as well to my church family, Flowing Rivers International Church for being such a tower of strength for me. My adopted family the Aviles as well as my adopted son, Carlos Ditren and soon to be Niece, Yessica Liriano, thank you for your wisdom and support.

Prologue

Before you begin reading this book, allow me to warn you: You will be challenged! My dear brother and sister, if you feel satisfied with your relationship with God, this book is not for you. Because within these pages you will discover a combination of two things: the testimony of the direct intervention of Almighty God in the life of a believer who hopes for and wants more of God, and an instrument to impart the same in your life.

This book Except The Lord along with the essence of verse from Psalm 127:1; has as an objective the goal of allowing us see in whom we must trust, hope and depend.

We should depend on the blessings of God and not on our own strength to build a house as opposed to expending our own strength to the point of exhaustion.

I believe God desires to rise up each believer in order for him to advance towards the purpose for which they were created. For this reason, each believer in Christ needs to move to a level and this level is total surrender to the will of God.

I believe that the book you have in your hands has been divinely anointed as an instrument to help you reach that level. It could be that you have not gone through a dramatic life experience as in the life of Dr. Terika Smith, but if you give God freedom to work in your life the way He wants, you will reach that level. That is the will of God.

This book is about you and your passion to understand life. It is about the search for control over the circumstances and your destiny. It is about living life to the fullest and reconnecting to your inner you. You have not been created to only exist but rather to live a life of great importance. This book refers to that life: Your life!

My prayer is that when you read this book, you receive the complete understanding of Except The Lord.

Bishop Juan Núñez R.
Pastor Centro Cristiano Camino de la Salvación

CONTENT
With Gratitude

Prologue .... Pg 5

Introduction .... Pg 9

The Perfect Storm .... Pg 13

Artifacts #1 .... Pg 21
   Random Thoughts Before The Storm .... Pg 19

Artifacts #2 .... Pg 31
   Lord Make Me Over .... Pg 33

Breaking Ground Phase I .... Pg 39
   Womb or Tomb .... Pg 41
   Groundbreaking .... Pg 47

Artifact #3 .... Pg 67
   Before The Build .... Pg 69

Artifact #4 .... Pg 77
   Thoughts From a Message:
   "I've Been Exposed – Who am I?" .... Pg 79

Building and Shaping Phase II .... Pg 87
   Peace .... Pg 89
   The Underlying Rock .... Pg 95
   Jesus at the Center .... Pg 103

Artifact #5 .... Pg 111
   Waiting .... Pg 113

Dedication and Possession Phase III . . . . . Pg 117
   Lord Bless This House . . . . Pg 119
   Everywhere You Go . . . . Pg 123
   Faith to Rise . . . . Pg 129

Artifact #6 . . . . Pg 133
   Still I Rise. . . . . Pg 135

Lessons Learned: Final Phase IV . . . . Pg 139
   It Was Good That I Had Been Afflicted . . . . Pg 141
   God Blocked It . . . . Pg 147
   Finding Your Inner Peace . . . . Pg 151
   Reference. . . . . Pg 153

Except the Lord builds a house, they labor in vane that build it, except the Lord keeps the city the watchman wakes in vane.

Psalm 127:1KJV

If God doesn't build the house, the builders only build shacks.
Psalm 127:1 Msg. Bible

Introduction

We go through life working hard towards accomplishing a goal that has no name, no face, and no point of origin, just a goal. We have been taught through society and in our own homes that we must work hard. We must make sure we position ourselves to succeed. The challenge is what defines working hard? What defines positioning ourselves to succeed? That has been a sticking point for me because the definition of working hard and succeeding are not constant for every person. What that looked like for our parents may not equate to what it looks like for my siblings, or me for you, or your siblings.

For my parents, working hard meant long hours, long days and sometimes three jobs to make sure everything was in order for their family. They modeled the value of having a lot and cherishing it, and having nothing and valuing it more. Paul said in Philippians 4:11-13 *"Not that I was ever in need, for I have learned how to get along happily whether I have much or little. I know how to live on almost nothing or everything. I have learned the secret of living in every situation, whether it is with a full stomach or empty, with plenty or little. For I can do everything with the help of Christ who gives me the strength I need."* They taught us not to get excited over money, wealth, or fame because as quickly as you get it, it can also go away. They looked at working hard as being intentional, having a goal in mind. They put in the hours now with hopes of retirement in the latter days.

By definition, to succeed is to achieve a desired aim or result. What does that mean? If you place five people in a room and ask them to give a definition of the word, they might all regurgitate the same response but none, or a few really, are able to provide a response with practical application. Growing up, my parents defined it as being better than they were, a tall order to fill. Sometimes I reflect and think that's unfair. The kind of parents that we are blessed to have made it a challenge, at least for me, to ever be able to fill those shoes. You will hear more about my parents in the section on foundation.

I am 44 years old and find myself in a place of quandary, juxtaposed between who I am, what is the plan of God for my life, and the foundation that shaped and is shaping me. I find myself stuck on a simple verse repeated time and again but has now taken up meaning in my life. Have I been laboring in vain? Is God or has God built my home? The writing of this book comes at the heel of probably the most exhausting perfect storm in my life. If I could disappear off the face of the earth I would and not return, but God.

The humility of serving God has convicted me in understanding that He is the architect and builder, the foundation upon, and in which, I must rest. I unequivocally cannot move forward. I cannot take another step in life or in the ministry without the confident assurance that God has built my house.

Through the Pastors and Leaders Conference hosted by my distant spiritual father, Bishop TD Jakes, I have learned not only from him but other greats like Pastor Paula White, "I got my bounce back," and Pastor Sheryl Brady "You have it in you," among others. This book and the many more to come is a reflection of the ministry that has been sedentary for too long and God had to allow me to go through my trials, and believe me they are not over, but I am resting in Jesus, in order for me to share myself with the many Terika's out there who need this word of encouragement to recharge their batteries and move forward.

God has blessed me over the years, to serve in a variety of capacities and hold multiple degrees. I have served as classroom teacher, school administrator, track coach, college professor, mentor and now pastor among other things. I am mother, daughter, sister and friend. My journey has afforded me exposure to so much of life that at this juncture, I am pause with determination to build meaning, release the buried baggage and allow the positioning that God has begun in my life to propel me into the purpose for which I have been placed on this earth. In my current role as Pastor, my hunger is to be more like Jesus knowing so many look to me, they look to my life for guidance on how to spread their spiritual wings and fly. This has caused me to become intentional and determined in my service to the kingdom of God.

I am determined not to be the Pastor who stands and regurgitates scripture to a body that need application. I am determined, as God continuously reveals to me, to be transparent with the Word of God and allow the truth of the purpose of my existence to be reflected wherever I go. I am determined that God will build my "house", such that title, degree, position, or power will not have an impact on the purpose of my existence. *If there is one thing I have learned it is that the attitude we portray internally and externally dictates the influence we have on those around us.* You don't have to be arrogant to get people to notice you, just be you, stand tall and never let another think of themselves more than that which is in you. The word of God says "Greater is he who is in us than he who is in the world." That being said, Devil I know what I have now more than before so find another tree.

Before I can take you into my newfound revelation and how God is building my house and wants to build yours, permit me to share a bit about my past. I will proceed with caution knowing that a lot of this will be new to even my parents, the skeletons in my closet that suppressed my voice for a long time until now. The first chapter, Random thoughts before the storm, is an inside to my rambling on looking for answers to questions spoken and unspoken.

The Perfect Storm

I watched a movie once titled The Perfect Storm. It was a movie about avid fishermen who were on the hunt for that perfect location for the perfect catch. They were to be the best of the best. They were excellent at what they did. Whether fishing, steering a boat or riding the rough waters, they knew how to handle themselves when out at sea at least until the perfect storm. These men found themselves in the heart of the perfect storm. The waves came from all directions. They were huge; they were ferocious and very unforgiving. The look in their eyes when they knew they were not going to make it out of this one alive. One by one they conceded to their fate. One by one they parted ways. One by one they, who were among the best at what they did, had to surrender to a force that was greater than them. Perfect storms are not intended to leave survivors only casualties.

The thing about perfect storms is the attack comes from all directions. It is not the case where you are hit from one direction, you handle it and then you move on bracing for the next attack. Neither is it the case where you are hit from two directions, a bit more challenging than only one direction nevertheless it is manageable with time and perseverance. With the perfect storm, the watch is synchronized. It can be compared to being on position to run a race and awaiting the starter to blow the whistle. Once the whistle blows, once the synchronized watch hits its intended hour, all wheels are in motion. The blows come from the north, the south, the east and the west all at the same time.

There is no escape. The target trapped in this storm is not on the outskirts but in the epicenter of the storm. Some would call this epicenter the eye of the storm.

In 2014, I found myself in a perfect storm. Every area of my life was under attack at the same time. The signs in each of these areas were there. *The build up was evident. Over and over again there were announcements, the weatherman of life kept signaling that something was about to happen.* The atmosphere in my life was no longer sunny. For close to a year, I lived in a gray cloud. Hovering over my life, my home, my ministry, my finances, my health, my very existence, it was hovering as though to consume me. It was a moment where I truly did not know which direction to turn in nor on whom to call for help. I was entering into a storm that had a beginning before my existence and was about to manifest itself in such a way that I wasn't sure how I was going to make it out of this one.

I have had storms in my life, storms as a young girl, storms as a teenager, and storms as a woman. I have had storms around my identity and the purpose of my existence. I have had storms in my finances, a loving and giving heart I had yet I couldn't seem to look back in my rainy days. I remember one day in church during a Wednesday night bible study I shared with those there that I was determined to break the spirit of poverty. I actually fasted to break it, it was a cycle God revealed that it did not matter how much money I made I was not going to continue the path that I was on. Countless have been blessed from my pocket but I had little to show for myself. So I was plummeted during this storm.

I was hit in the area of relationships, people who surrounded me and befriended me were turned in such a way that I was in a cocoon. I wasn't sure how I got into it but I know nothing goes into a cocoon and come out the same. But it was a storm. I can't say it was easy. I lost relationships that hugged and kissed, and laughed. Was any of it real? The church I pastored was no longer the place for me to minister and worship. It became a place that I now understand was a womb. My storm ripped me out, pushed me out of the womb I resided in for 5 ½ years. The birthing process is a painful one and so was this separation. The storm for me was the impact of the amino sack being ripped open and life coming forth, never to feed again on the resources, the nutrients of its former host.

Samuel did not begin his journey until he was weaned from his mother Hannah and released into his purpose. I am eternally grateful to the host that carried me, the church that birthed me, as I would not have been released into my purpose if there were not a place from which to be released. The perfect storm was in part the byproduct of a divine positioning where the pain I would be entering into was a shift designed by God. You will never get to where God wants you if you remain comfortable in a host that no longer has room for you.

This perfect storm came after the nucleus of my home. It was not enough my finances, my ministry, and my relationships. Now I see where my home was being turned upside down. Love was seemingly being ripped out of our fiber. The harmony of our unity that brought us together was a shadow and there was nothing I could do to address it but pray and hold fast to God's hands. I knew love was there but the cloud was really thick. It was to the point where for the first time, I internalized things so greatly that I was hospitalized for observation. I was not speaking. I was not releasing. *The magnitude of this perfect storm in my life literally shook the foundation of who I was and I no longer knew who I was.* At least that was how I felt at the time. I was the strong one, every one looked to me for direction but who did I look to. But God!

This perfect storm in 2014 lead to great revelation of hidden things, past hurt, concealed pain that connected to the why of me today. There was a need to reflect, no really reflect so that God could do what he was about to do in my life. The only way I was going to make it out of this perfect storm alive was by going through the process and letting God be God. I had a Job moment.
    I felt God gave Satan permission to go to work on me. I felt

like there was no way, knowing how much I love Him that God would allow all of this to happen to me unless he trusted I would make it through. I guess he remembered the song I used to sing. "*I love Him too much to turn back now, I love Him too much to break my vow, I promised the Lord I would make it somehow, I love Him too much to turn back* now." It came from my heart and He trusted my word.

This book, as I write, is not because I pretend to have all the answers nor is it a manual of how to. This is an opportunity for me to share a burden and a word of encouragement to all reading, especially anyone in ministry, who find themselves trying to be perfect in an imperfect world. You want to do the best for the Lord yet you are challenged on every end. This is not to say the challenges are wrong. I have learned and continue to learn that this call is truly a road less traveled. If you mean business for Jesus you will go through the Job moments. For my readers who may not understand a "Job moment," I am referring to the biblical character named Job. He was a righteous and honorable man who did no wrong yet God saw it fit to allow Satan to bring harm to all he had except take his life. For more understanding I encourage you to read the Book of Job in the Old Testament. The only way God will know he can trust you is to watch what you do as you go through. Will you grow through or will you give up. He knows your heart but do you? This book is for those who, like myself have been called by God to be used by Him for His glory. That being said, you will go through fire, pass through floods, endure great persecution and as Paul says, "having done all to stand."

This book is for the minister who is willing to become transparent enough with their congregation to allow them to not refer to us as abstract but tangible. **Too many want to sit at the head table but have never visited the kitchen.** Too many want to be served and have never served before. Transparency has helped my messages become more real to those listening. They can see that I understand their pain and I can relate to their pain. **Except the Lord** was birthed out of a perfect storm that should have left me for dead but instead has propelled me into my destiny. If God is not the builder of our being meaning everything about us then we are positioning ourselves to live in shacks that will crumble at the slightest wind. I don't sing, *"I know who I am, I am yours and you are mine"* because it is a song. I know who I am, it took a perfect storm but I do. Do you?

This book is for the parent who may be struggling with their parenting skills. Am I doing this right? Or, what am I doing wrong? This journey spoke to me on the fact that while there were areas to change, there were other areas where God was saying, "That part belongs to me." It's like the writer says, "After you have done all you can, you stand." As parents it is easy to feel like a failure. My challenge, as I have learned and so I write is, have you? Have you failed? As you read, see if God was not allowing this journey to reveal some things and eradicate others so that you could stand whole and complete before God. As you read, learn to shed and learn to celebrate. Let God build!

This book is for the individual who cannot give reason to why their "now" situation or circumstance is not reflective of where they want to be. Why are they unable to break past the invisible barrier that seems to be thwarting their progress? Why is it so hard to really be happy and content? What is weighing them down? What is that "it factor"? You may not get the direction you need here but you will embark upon a process, a road you must travel.

Random thoughts before the storm: February 21, 2014 10:31pm

Random thoughts are just that, thoughts that flowed from my mind early in 2014 as I found myself in the wind of the brewing storm. These are thoughts that brought me to a place of understanding that I had deep hidden wounds that were untouched. In other words, I had wounds that were buried under the foundation of my being. These were things that were never discussed but left a scar. These were things that were contaminating my thoughts, my actions, my attitude and at points, my ministry. Sometimes, society expects you as a pastor to walk a line of perfection that is unjust. I say unjust because, at least in my case, I felt buried within myself. There was no room for error and worse, no room to be human before the ones you must shepherd. You are supposed to have all the answers.

This particular night I found myself enthralled in a sea of emotions. Actually, this was one of many over the years but the first where I felt so overwhelmed where disappearing was an actualizing thought. I began a journal entry that would take me as far back as my infancy. **You cannot move into who you are to become unless you face the tombs beneath your concrete, the hidden things.**

ARTIFACT ENTRY #1

Its funny, all of my life I had great dreams of something I couldn't even describe, I couldn't put my hand on it. I knew I was a dreamer. I spent hours daydreaming. What's even scarier is that my daydreaming seemed so real. That was my escape from my boring life. I had responsibilities. I cooked, I cleaned, I went to school, and I went to church. With my parents permission I visited my friends from time to time but not for long. Basically my life was a routine that was my norm, a norm I now find to be really boring. Funny, my mom would say that when I was younger I was really quiet. She would say that she was concerned about me because I was such an introvert. I am not sure when or to what age she was referring.

What I know is my past is so silent, so hidden that if it had not been for the love of The Lord, I am not sure I would be here right now. In fact I know I would not be here right now. I would be or should be lost, confused, caught in a life of the forgotten. God, what am I talking about? I sometimes am not sure. I think a lot of this is surfacing now as I am raising a 19-year-old young lady who I love to the core but sometimes I wonder if I love her more than she can handle or I can offer. I don't know. I find that I am doing to her what I know, raising her the way I was raised, loving her openly a lot more than I received. I guess I don't want her to struggle, held hostage to her past like I was. I declare that although I know there is so much I have not said out loud, I refuse to let my yesterday hold me captive today. **I refuse to let yesterdays terrors rob me of today's blessings.** *I guess that's what I am trying to teach her. I see her and I see me in many ways. When I look at her, the only difference between us aside from the age is the fight. I didn't fight love; I didn't fight having someone who would so willingly want to spend time. I was older before my mom started asking me personal questions, that I can recall and not to mention my dad. Dad loved me "estilo daddy" his way. It was a way I could not understand. It was hard. It was scary at times. It was serious. I knew he loved me and still does but he was never the one to really give the pampering that I think I needed. I love him. I find my self now being father and mother to my daughter, but it's hard. I think it is hard because the kind of love that I know of is not* the kind I think she wants or needs. It sucks because I try not to be Pastora with her. I try to not be Dr. Smith with her. I try to just be me but how can I be me when me is trying to figure out who that is. It sucks.

The question that I have to answer is simply who am I? I have been more actively asking that question since the days of my dissertation when I wrote a poem asking that question. I have to be able to answer it because then and only then will I get to my core. I want to get to my core. I preach. I teach. I parent. I lead. That is not my core. I love God. He is my center and my world. So why do I do all of what I do? I see myself helping people. I see myself helping a lot of people. I see myself connecting to people like me. But who am I? Who the heck am I?

When I look back, I have lots of hurts, most of which I have told no one, but why?

Being just a little girl and having a grown man pull me outside of the house, when no one would suspect and fondle me. I remember it, its as clear as day. He was a soldier, I remember he was a big guy; of course, I was a kid so everyone was big at that time. Why me? Why did he need to touch my innocence? Why didn't I tell anyone? Why didn't I scream? I guess I felt it was okay. I didn't experience any pain and besides, what was I doing out there? I was just a little girl.

I might have been around six years old and in bed. My family was there. Some people were visiting. It was bedtime. I am asleep and then I feel the pressure. What was that all about? Why is this adult, a grown man on top of me. Not just that, the pain, I had the panic but the sound did not come out. Why not? Was it because it was someone close to the family? I wasn't more than 6 years old. That was wrong. I never told anyone, but I hurt.

I think I was 8 when I was walking home from school and out of nowhere an army jeep came speeding down the street. I woke up in the hospital. They patched me up and sent me home. But how could they have missed the rock. It was a good size rock that was wedged in my side. Are you kidding me? The scar is there today. My mom was my medical hero. That rock, hidden under my panties wedged in my side was no different than the cruelty of that man and the other adult.

I hurt growing up. I now see more that that longing to figure me out began early in my youth and I had no understanding of why. Anything that is worth cherishing is treated with care. My family loved me. My family cared for me. They did not know that I was tormented inside. They did not know that my innocence was robbed. It was wrong. I guess it made me not only withdrawn but also a tough silent river that was not to be messed with. I don't know.

It hurt coming to this country and being misunderstood. Being fat, ugly, unwelcomed and unwanted. One day I was even called half human, well they were not wrong at the time because my childhood experience surely was not human or humane. The bible says when father and mother forsake me The Lord will lift me up. Boy is that the truth. My parents never forsook me, they just didn't know where I was and the torment I was in, but God. He is the one who lifted me up and who is still lifting me up today. I remember when I was in the sixth grade, they called me ape and gorilla and for entertainment, I would growl like one and chase kids around. That wasn't who I was but that was what I was becoming, a cheap thrill for insensitive 6th graders who did not know better.

It hurt being in school, high school now and you are dressed in white and kids throw food at you. Imagine you in the cafeteria. Its bad enough not many will sit with you but to have mean kids throw food at you, it's hard. Lord as I remember and the wounds are being scratched, thank you for taking me through.

It hurts to work hard and then because you are credentialed no guy with a degree will look at you and worse one without. It's crazy. You would think a brother would want a smart woman but all I hear is that you are intimidating. What? You just can't handle me.
 You just don't have enough intestinal fortitude to love me for

me. It hurts. Why should I apologize for the fight I went through to prepare myself and for the places God has taken me just because you are insecure, the devil is a lie. It hurts.

It hurts to feel alone. I live in a house with two amazing people; really the family God has given me. I love them. They love me but we don›t talk. We have gotten to a place of coexisting in the same space. It's wrong. I am being ripped inside and the truth, the thought crossed my mind will they miss me when I am gone? Will they miss me at all? If when I am here they acknowledge not each other let alone me, what if I were not here. Don't get me wrong, I love my life too much to be stupid and do something with it. As Bishop TD Jakes says, if anyone says that I took my life its a lie. I go when God takes me, period. But would they miss me? It hurts.

It hurts when the one friend that I thought I had; my sister went MIA for one whole year. Really? Who does that? She is my sister, my friend, and the one I thought I could talk to. Not having her around caused me to retreat again into my hole. I had my little one, who I cant even call that anymore, I stand corrected, but I at least could talk with her about topical stuff. Wow, where is the love? It hurts.

It hurts to know that I am not getting any younger and I have so much to give but not sure where to or who to give it to. I want to give love to a child. I have Karen but she is pushing me away. Not sure I will go the parenting route again so what now. I cannot fathom starting over, I cant fathom raising another child, I don›t know. What now? It hurts. I don›t think I can have children plus heck, I›m 43, 44 in a few months so who am I fooling. I am not married, not sure when that will be. I am just hoping in God for another day. That's really all I can do. Now what? It sucks and it hurts.

I remember as a young girl my sister and my mom would joke about how I would always try to rescue people, who do I rescue or better yet, who rescues me? This is crazy. This hurts. What now? What is my mission, what is my purpose, why do I exist?

25

When I look in the mirror of life I am seeing definitions associated with titles but are they who I am to be or a byproduct of that reality?

I am a pastor; I have a body of believers that God is going to hold me accountable for. How do I do that? I know I can't by myself, He has to help me, and he has to lead me. He has to guide me, every step of the way. That's my constant plea, Lord I can't do this, everything that this represents, I can't do without you. The crazy thing is that I tell God whatever he is going to do, don›t do it without me. Okay, what's wrong with that picture? I am bold enough to say yes because I do trust Him but a scared child on the inside to not let him down. What have I gotten myself into?

God has allowed me to do so much, see so much, experience, so much. There has been a whole lot of good and a whole lot of bad. Something, something he can use me for. **I am a far cry from where I was yet I know that the core of me, the purpose of my existence is still to be unfolded.** I want it to happen. I want to see what he will do with me. I am concerned about losing my mama (Karen) and my big guy (nephew) in the process. I put them in God›s hands. I know they love each other but this time, I can't take them on.

The chest pains are becoming more real each and every day. I don›t like to talk about them but they are real. The more I can get myself to not yell, not try to force an issue and just calm myself down, trusting that God is in control the better I will be. I know there is much to be done and I have to be healthy to get it done.

I did not go through what I went through as a child to not be able to help someone today, someone whose voice has been silent or silenced. No, I can't sit idly by. Lord, what is my core, the purpose of my existence, the why I get up in the mornings?

After reading my ramblings I realize just how far God has brought me. As mentioned above, the night that I rambled on, I had reached a place of inner desperation, trying to find the why things were unfolding the way they were and connect them to who

I am becoming. As a Pastor, you do not have all the answers especially when you accept the fact that you too have journeyed and you are endlessly on the potter's wheel. If anything, this reflection and others to come have helped me in my current state to stand more firmly rooted in purpose. My constant quest is replete with questions but all answers leading back to the one text, "except the Lord builds the house." Just that alone helps me to not only reflect back but also look forward as I share my healing journey with you the reader.

As I look back, I am not sure I would have arrived at this place had it not been for the perfect storm. In the movie, the best of the best had to face that which was greater than them. They had gone into territory that was not theirs and they were not coming out alive. The difference, I find, is that this storm by my self would yield the same fate. However, I serve a God who IS greater. ***I entered the storm due to decisions I made and many made for me yet it would serve to reveal the hidden roots, remove the heavy weights and allow me to face today with a tenacity I never knew I had.***

I shared my thoughts because although revealing, I hope it can inspire others to trust God enough to be transparent with Him. He already knows us but he is waiting for us to release ourselves totally in Him.

In the next chapter, I share a poem I had written in early 2000 while completing my doctoral studies. Who would have thought how relevant a poem written then would be to where I am in my life today? It goes to show our quest for purpose, our quest for understanding is not an overnight cerebral explosion. Polonius, in Shakespeare's Hamlet Hamlet Act 1, scene 3, 78–82 says the following:

> *This above all: to thine own self be true,*
> *And it must follow, as the night the day,*
> *Thou canst not then be false to any man.*

Farewell, my blessing season this in thee!

There are too many who go through life preaching, teaching and winning accolades for the profound accomplishments of their external man while on the inside they are lost, confused and dishonest to themselves and society. **To be transparent is to become vulnerable.** To be transparent is to become susceptible to societal ridicule. This much I know, in the midst of the vulnerability and the societal ridicule, if you are true to yourself there is not an opposing force that can make you fall. The writer in Psalms 92:12-13 NKV says:

> [12] *The righteous shall flourish like the palm tree: he shall grow like a cedar in Lebanon.* [13] *Those that be planted in the house of the LORD shall flourish in the courts of our God.*

The conviction I have within is simply this. I have been called to the noblest call in life, serving God. When He called me He already knew who I was and where he was taking me, I needed to figure it out for myself. God, the Alpha and the Omega, is already at my finish line cheering me to walk towards him. I write now as one who has journeyed further along the continuum of the call towards the purpose of my existence, the purpose of the call. The more true I am with myself, the more real God becomes in me, the more people to whom I will be able to minister.

My journey continues to teach me that the more true I am to myself the more opposition I might face but rooted and grounded like the palm tree whose roots are wrapped around the rock, I will bend but I will not break. I will face opposition but it will not destroy me. The more true I am to myself I will stand like the Cedars of Lebanon, tall and strong, intimidating to their enemies. It is believed that the Cedars of Lebanon grew to be about 120 feet high and about 30 feet in diameters. That being the case, to reach that height and width takes time. Lebanon is known for its harsh climates, sandstorms, humidity, seasonal rain, and unbearable temperatures. Taking that into account, as the Psalmist compares us to palm trees and Cedar Trees of Lebanon, there is an implication of strength, resilience, a firm foundation and purpose. In Mathew 7:24-27 NKV Jesus says,

> [24] *Therefore whosoever heareth these sayings of mine, and doeth them, I will liken him unto a wise man, which built his house upon a rock:*
>
> [25] *And the rain descended, and the floods came, and the winds blew, and beat upon that house; and it fell not: for it was founded upon a rock.*
>
> [26] *And every one that heareth these sayings of mine, and doeth them not, shall be likened unto a foolish man, which built his house upon the sand:*
>
> [27] *And the rain descended, and the floods came, and the winds blew, and beat upon that house; and it fell: and great was the fall of it.*

I want to believe that the strength of the Palm Tree and the Cedars of Lebanon rest on the foundation that is set on, wrapped around, rooted in the rock. When the storms of Lebanon come, they are not moved, the palm might bend but it rises up again after the storm.

ARTIFACT ENTRY #2

Lord, Make Me Over

Embarking upon this journey has really helped me to realize that I have been looking for God to make me over for some time now, I just didn't know how to begin the process. I just didn't know the path. I remember while in the doctoral program, in one of my classes I had to write a poem of expression looking at the inner journey of man as it related to where I was. This would later become a part of my final dissertation in the program. As I read and reread the poem, this truly has been my age-old question, who am I?

Who am I?
From Sullivan to Evanston
I took the train, the bus, my mom's Volkswagen
On that cold October day
Lord don't let the cops stop me I pray
Oh no! I was kicked out of school
Because I acted a fool
Trying to prove myself
I took the gun off the shelf

Visited my boy Big Busta
You **know** he's a gangsta
In the hood is where he stayed
Let **me** tell you how I got played
My girl Raven
Got a bun in the oven
I told the teacher
She reminds me of a preacher
But she cared enough
She didn't reveal my stuff
I wasn't doing well in class
She worked with me to pass
School was no place for fools
Said she as she equipped me with the tools
To make a decision
To live right and have ambition
One day in class
She told me about her past

She said

When I left for the university
I encountered a lot of adversity
In the classroom
And the game room

You see

I was never smart
Nor did I play the part
Of one who knew enough
To ask the question
What will enhance my progression?
My focus became clearer
As graduation date drew nearer
In nineteen ninety three

I was employed by Palatine you see
Spanish was my main area
But I found myself in a bind
When I realized
That I was hypnotized
By the notion
Of my purpose and devotion
To being a teacher
Not a preacher
Who cared a lot
To find a spot
In each kid's life
As they deal with strife
Of this world in which they live
They always have to give

Up

Man woman child
All filled with pride
One black one white
During the day or at night
The race has started
The race has started
Can we heal the broken hearted?
Whose race gender or intellect
Forces them to reflect
On the defining factor
Of their character

Man, who am I?

From construction in ma's womb
To deconstruction in the tomb
To reconstruction in the minds of those
Who remember my life in prose

The story behind this poem was the life of one of my former students who found himself in a sticky situation with his then girlfriend. He confided in me sharing the struggles of being in the hood and the fight for survival, wanting to get out and feeling stuck. When we spoke, I realized that my life may have been different but I too was in the same quandary of who I was. It ended with the three guarantees of our existence: born out of a womb, die and bury in a tomb and be constantly evaluated in the minds of those you come in contact with.

As I write, I find the Holy Spirit leading me to return to this original point of questioning. Without knowing that this day would come where I would be writing so transparently to you my reading audience. Out of that perfect storm mentioned earlier, the Lord has set me on a journey of self-discovery. It was prudent for Him that I knew who I was in order to understand whose I was. It was important for him that I understood the power of my inheritance and knows how to use it. Many people get their inheritance and waste it. There is no added value to it. They did not have to pay a price for it. My inheritance is not material wealth. It cannot be bought. The only way I could truly claim it is by understanding my right standing in the family.

God spoke to Israel through Jeremiah saying,
in Jeremiah 29:10-11,

> *10 For thus saith the LORD, That after seventy years be accomplished at Babylon I will visit you, and perform my good word toward you, in causing you to return to this place.*
>
> *11 For I know the thoughts that I think toward you, saith the LORD, thoughts of peace, and not of evil, to give you an expected end.*

God spoke to Israel through Jeremiah and before telling them that he had a plan for them and it was good and not evil, he told them they would have to go through something. This path of self discovery and questioning, I have found is my "something" that God had to allow me to go through that I can now stand tall and say, here I am Lord, you can send me where you want me to go. You can use me how you want to use me. I am all yours. God told Jeremiah tell them, that they would first go through 70 years of captivity and then he will take them out and give them their promise.

The rest of the book will be broken into Phases: **Breaking Ground**, **Building and Shaping**, **Dedication** and **Possession**. As I am writing the Lord is reminding me of the metamorphosis of the butterfly. **Romans 12:2** *And be not conformed to this world: but be ye transformed by the renewing of your mind, that ye may prove what is that good, and acceptable, and perfect, will of God.* It is impossible for a butterfly to take flight without a prior sacrifice made. The caterpillar had to sacrifice its shape, way of living and even appearance to make room for a new way of life. If God is not allowed to build our house we will remain caterpillars for life. We will become comfortable in our surroundings and comfortable in our environment. There will be an unwillingness to endure the pain of change to see the potential of our purpose. We will not fly unless we first die. As we move forward into this book, I share how much of me had to die and how much of anyone desirous of growing in Christ will have to die if we are to fly.

BREAKING GROUNDPHASE I

Womb or Tomb?

One of my favorite movies of all time is the Lion King. You probably thought because I am a pastor I was going to go deep. The truth is I am really not that deep. In fact my conviction with this book is to keep it real. I'll save the intellectual jargon for the next book. I love the Lion King because it portrays the cycle of life, birth – growth – separation – restoration – birth. It is a continuous cycle. Simba thought he could abandon the plan for his life by running away from his community after he felt himself guilty of the death of his father, Mufasa. He tried to take on a new life in a new environment until destiny caught up with him. It took one visit, a reminder of who he was. His mask was an image but not the reality of who he was. His two friends didn't even know who he was because he tried to forget who he was. **Sometimes we go through life wearing an image, trying to fit into a life that is not who we are.** It's like when you confess Jesus as your Lord, you try to do the things your friends do but you are never at peace. You are never a fit. You are a misfit. God has put up every roadblock to shield you from you. Simba found himself having to come to terms with who he was and making the most important decision of his life. He would return home, face his demons and defend his destiny. He would become the King of Pride Land, walking in the shoes of Mufasa.

The womb is a place where history begins and where history is perpetuated. Within the womb a new life is formed and incubated and out of it a new life is birthed, the cycle continues. Anthropologists have a difficult time agreeing on a definition of culture, however, what is consistent is that culture is not something you are born with but what you learn along the way. Our foundation is therefore acquired as a result of our exposure.

In the 1920's the story broke of the two young girls who were being raised by wolves.

"One of the most well-documented cases of children raised by wild animals is that of Kamala and Amala, better known as the "wolf children." *Discovered in 1920 in the jungles of Godamuri, India, the girls, aged 3 and about 8, had been living with a she-wolf and her pack. It's not known if the girls were from the same family, but the man who found the girls, Reverend J.A.L. Singh, took them back to his orphanage, where he tried to get them accustomed to their human surroundings. While the girls made some progress over the years, both eventually came down with fatal illnesses, leaving the reverend* to wonder *"if the right thing to do would have been to leave these children in the wild where I found them."*

It is hard to pluck someone out of an environment where they have been all their lives and introduce them to a new one without expecting adverse reactions of sorts.

I grew up in a loving home. I had parents and three other siblings, a sister who is the eldest, an older brother and a younger brother. They are each now adults and married. Each has given my parents two grandchildren totaling six. I am the only that is not yet married but God has blessed me with my nutcracker, Karen. My parents proudly celebrate their seven grandchildren. I am thankful. My parents who are now pastoring a church in Florida, my father a Bishop and mother a Reverend, have reached a place in their lives where they are catching a second wind and are serving God with a fire and zeal as I have never before seen. Our lives were not so growing up.

As a child, I was very quiet. I didn't speak much but as you learned before, I experienced a lot. Whether that was the reason for my quiet stage I cannot say. What I can say is now a parent; I see where I had a wish list of if my parents could, then maybe. If I could have engaged in some of the life questions then maybe I would have had a better self-esteem. If I heard more "I love you" growing up, maybe I wouldn't crave it as much as I do today. Do not misunderstand; I have no sincere regrets because I was only being formed in God's perfect plan. My childhood had been filled with many happy moments. My parents exposed us to life preparing us to navigate any circle without being "frightened" (meaning lose our mind because they are human just like us) when surrounded by people in position. The scripture that sums up my earlier years with my parents is as the Apostle Paul says in Philippians 4:12-13 *"I know how to be abased, and I know how to abound. Everywhere and in all things I have learned both to be full and to be hungry, both to abound and to suffer need. *¹³* I can do all things through Christ*[a] *who strengthens me."* In Jamaica, my father was a very high ranking official in the Jamaican Defense Force so we were a family that was exposed to life. We were blessed. Yes discipline was strict. We grew up under very heavy hands; a look was all we needed. We were taught discipline times two. If the civilian family was well disciplined, the children of Regimental Sargent Major, Smith needed to be more disciplined and well mannered. Yes, it was love, tough and perfect, as they knew how.

Later I refer to how I was raising my nutcracker and realizing my wineskin could not become hers. In Jamaica, I was the child of a high-ranking military official. Here in America, I was the daughter of a former high ranking military official now security guard and technician. Our geographical positioning changed but it did not deter our parents from the continued exposure to life. The difference, however, was that we had to begin learning a new language. We still spoke English but the American culture had a language system that, if not careful can cause you to lose the person you were when leaving your country. In my case, it did in several ways. I became even more reserved, did not have a lot of friends and accepted treatment that would never have been tolerable in Jamaica. *It was change but thank God for my parents who never released us to our fears but exposed us to our potential.*

From my mom, I am tender and nurturing. I am also a bit trusting, always hoping that even the most blatantly wicked person could change. We have a more patient love in the Lord and his mercy. From my dad, I am aggressively strong. I can put my hand down hard and stick to it. I am a living witness for all those who are trying to shed some generational traits, if you pray and ask God to remove them, he will. I have watched God remove some of my dad's traits from me because I have prayed. I would catch myself wanting to just give a person a new life when I realize they are taking advantage of me. I now have my mom's reaction. I pray for them and show them a love that can sometimes become confusing because I should be helping them to their casket.

The thing about the womb experience is that it's a place, as mentioned before for incubation of life but there comes a time when the life that is within must come out. This is the time when the life has overstayed its welcome. It is of age. It's purpose of being there to grow limbs, organs, and eventual independence has now moved to another plane and someone must go. A mother who is pregnant will have to release the baby otherwise her life and the baby's life will be jeopardized. I have learned in life that this scenario is not only for the natural womb of a mother. A person can go through the same experiences while on the job or in the home. Beginning with the home, as your children get older, their attitudes and behavior are demonstration that the environment and rules that once guided them are of no more effect. It is time for them to move on to a different environment for the next phase of their lives. The challenges in the home and strain on the relationships are not because of lost love but expired space. The space was great for growing but not adequate for shifting. It was great for crawling but not suitable for walking and then running.

On the job, we find that the journey of the child at home just described is the same. We get to a point in our career in a place where we have tapped out. There is no more potential for growth. Some stay because of fear of change and others because of control. Change can mean new learning and new environment and with age and a generational shift of tech babies those who did not grow up on that software maybe intimidated. On the other hand you might have those who love the control of being able to dominate the area they are in and not wanting to be lead by someone else with greater insight and in some cases more modern. These are the individuals who love status quo, don't create waves. The challenge with both if not addressed is that the environment will shift around them and they may find themselves the fixtures in the process of decay. For these, the womb is a tomb. It is not until something or someone intervenes that they realize their starting point was just incubation and not a dwelling place. Something has to open their eyes to understand they were not assigned there to stay, it was the path to the purpose of their earthly assignment.

As I considered the shift from womb to tomb, taking into context the text that is driving this work, I realize each day that sometimes God has to put you in a place for you to see what has been buried, the roots that are hindering your potential. He uses that place, that environment to point out the things you would otherwise overlook and to loose the things you are holding on to. Sometimes we want to be born but not let go of the umbilical chord. The only way to separate your past from your future is to cut the chord, that's painful. God was showing me that you could be constructed and deconstructed in the same environment because of your unwillingness to separate, take a step of faith, and take the plunge. When you look at a seed, it is the womb of the tree and the fruit potential inside but if you don't bury it, change its environment, it wont reach its potential of breaking to release what is inside of it. As we move forward, I share how God had to take this seed out of the environment it was in and position it in order to release the potential that was in it. While this environment was it was necessary, it was never intended to be permanent.

Groundbreaking

Genesis 2:7 "Then the Lord God formed a man from the dust of the ground and breathed into his nostrils the breath of life, and the man became a living being."

I would suppose that in life we go through many phases of groundbreaking. Moments in our lives where a shift occurs causing the ground beneath us to move. In some cases it might be a simple tremor while in others it is a radical move wherein everything that could possible hold you up seems to disappear, fall apart.

The earth shook beneath me as I transitioned into the American Public Schools. It was so different from Jamaica. In Jamaica we wore uniforms, everyone spoke the same way and no one judged you at least that's how I felt. When you are in the sixth grade in this country, everything looks differently. My mindset was also different because in Jamaica I had passed the Common Entrance Exam and was ready for high school at the early age of 10. It was a shock then to leave all that and arrive to a country of illusion only to encounter that the streets were not paved with gold. Everyone did not look the same nor sound the same. The worst part was to know that the ones who were from Jamaica were among the top to reject me. The transition was hard and isolating.

I have seen over the years how this experience helped shape my perspective on how I relate to immigrants. I now see my innate desire to rescue the rejected. Sometimes it is in my reflections that I gain strength to face the tough moments before me. I get a look over my shoulder moment, think things through moment and I realize the good out weigh the bad. I can't complain, I wont complain. It took me a while to get there though. Yet when you have been through as many shifts as I have and seen how God has kept me standing I truly can't complain. Lord thank you for the tremors and thank you for the ground falling apart, I wont complain. Thank you.

The groundbreaking that occurred in my life on the evening of September 22, 2014 was unprecedented. It was an earthquake like moment that on another day, in another season of my life would have resulted in casualties, myself included. The Bible says in 1 Peter 5:10 *"And the God of all grace, who called you to his eternal glory in Christ, after you have suffered a little while, will himself restore you and make you strong, firm and steadfast."* In my earlier ramblings, I share a significantly small portion of the challenges I have faced in life, that God has allowed me to endure all in preparation to the place I now find myself in. To get an idea of the type of shift I am referring to, I draw reference to the Great Chilean Earthquake. In 1960, Chile experienced the most powerful earthquake recorded in history. It came in at 9.5 on the Richter scale and lasted approximately 10 minutes. The result of this earthquake that only lasted 10 minutes had a tsunami effect that "affected southern Chile, Hawaii, Japan, the Philippines, eastern New Zealand, southeast Australia, and the Aleutian Islands." 10 minutes resulted in almost six thousand deaths and over six billion dollars in repairs.

On September 22, 2014 the clarity of my purpose of coming to MA became even clearer. This was the day that I ceased from being the Senior Pastor of the church that incubated me for 5 ½ years. Yes, that's it; it was the womb in which God would place me so that I could develop into the understanding of my purpose and my call. Praise God! It is now as I write that the clarity of the call has hit home. Pastor Paula White calls it "the clarion call". Let's start from the beginning.

My journey towards my purpose was accelerated during the summer of 2006 when I flew to Boston, MA for a second interview for the position as Principal for the International High School in Lawrence, MA. I served as principal for 4 ½ years to a wonderful team of teachers, administrators and most of all my babies, the students of INT. I will never forget my babies. Today I see them on the streets, in the stores, and at times in church and while I have forgotten a lot of names, the faces are in my heart. When I relocated to Lawrence, MA, I knew one of the key essentials for me would have been to identify a church home, a place to worship. Serving God was always important to me. My personal commitment to God was never about attending a building but finding a place to worship Him and with a body of people who loved Him. In my quest, I visited three churches, the third would become my home and eventually the one I would pastor for 5 ½ years, more on that later.

So what happened? When you have served God all of your adult life and some of your young adult life, you experience a lot. You get an understanding about people, the Word of God, the person of the Holy Spirit, and the love of God through the sacrifice of his son Jesus Christ. Now what you do with that information has to do with how you have applied the lessons learned along the way. I used to say my being in Massachusetts was Abramic in nature. Abraham along with his wife left all that they had, all that they knew and set out on a journey that was lead by God. He embarked on a walk of faith that was unprecedented. He trusted God.

When I left Illinois to begin a new life in MA, I understood I would be alone, though I did not know what that would look like. I literally left father, mother, siblings, family, everything that I knew and moved to a place I had only been once and that was a job interview. I had peace knowing that God was the one who hired me and that he would take care of me. I guess I was always weird like that, I knew my all was in God's hands so I would not be held captive by any man, position or title that would try to intimidate me into thinking they could make a decision on me at any time. I held close to the story of Job where as a man of God, Satan could not touch him unless God allowed him. I knew then and know now that I am a woman of God so no weapon formed against me yesterday, today, or tomorrow will ever prosper as long as God is on my side. Praise God!

I did what I knew for three years and then it happened. After trying to fill the position of Senior Pastor for the church where I attended, all eyes turned to me. Serving God always scared me just knowing my accountability was to Him. **Bottom line, I don't fear man, but I am terrified of God, in a good way.** Would you like to have God as your boss? I could never understand people who play in the pulpit because my mentality was like, do you know who your boss is? I mean, all he needs is a word. God has a way of speaking to people without asking your permission. Thank you Lord. The Lord had spoken in such a mighty way that when the time came for me to be introduced to the church, there was confirmation on all levels. Have you ever been so scared, if you had a clue you suddenly became clueless? I cried, I cried, and I cried. I knew it was God! I can play with a lot but not with God. I called my parents and their response just caused me to shake even more. I believe it was my dad who first answered, regardless, the first response was "serving God was the highest call we could ever have". I was done. I had two BAs, one MA, an Ed.D and a couple of certificates, none of that mattered anymore. I had become an embryo in a womb that would carry me for 5 ½ years.

What do you do when you are an accomplished professional doing what you think you have been called to do only to find that one day, one decision can shift your entire thinking? What do you do when 10 minutes could cost you over $6 billion as it did Chile? What do you do when the thing you are called to require more than you and no school exists that can prepare you for what you are about to enter into? What do you do when the best part is the culture is 180 degrees different from yours? I found myself pastoring a culture primarily Dominican and Puerto Rican. There were other cultures but the only one who looked or sound like me initially was me. What do you do? God, what are you up to? What do you know about me that I do not know? I found myself in a womb that would incubate me and prepare me for the next phase of my life in a way I could not understand. The icing on the cake is in my second year, I met a young lady who would not only ask me to be her godmother for her 15th birthday but in the plan of God would become her mother. My "nutcracker" as I fondly called her would enter my womb as I was in a womb. God you are funny!

Womb Within the womb

It was January 3, 2011 while I was in the office at the church when Karen, "nutcracker" entered with her mother, grandmother and brother. This was following a previous meeting where the decision for Karen's future would be that she would live with her mother and attend school in another district. I was surprised, scared and excited all in one because that visit shifted my life, another shift. I would become Karen's legal guardian and as of that moment she would live with me. I would be enrolling her in school. Yikes! I was a parent. Really God, are you serious? I was in a womb being incubated for a purpose and now I was becoming a womb for my nutcracker. I woke up single and childless and went to bed a single parent to an amazing, life changing 16-year-old daughter. Did I mention she is Puerto Rican?

I took her to the Woman Thou Art Loosed Conference where Bishop preached on the Pecking Order. It did not resonate with either of us then but it has become my go to now a couple years later. That preaching helped me understand the concept of the womb, the hiding place. I have more recently told her I now understand that I am her Rahab, strategically positioned in her life to be the gatekeeper of her anointing and she the protector of mine. My position in her life has served in many ways as a catapult of me wanting to understand God's word more. I figure if I am to be the servant of God that I am called to be, the mother

I have been called to be then I must at least try to understand the heart of the one who has called me. Wow!

In one shift, I moved from Principal to Pastor. In another shift I moved from living alone to parenting my daughter. God had begun a work in me the moment I said yes that I could not understand but am now putting the pieces together. I remember trying to put together a sermon in the last year before the earthquake of my life and found it near impossible. The text was simple, Psalms 127:1, the title of this book, Except The Lord. I could not answer what that meant. I could not explain what seemed to be such a logical text when I felt like I and all that was around me was not making any sense. Five years have passed since I said yes to leading God's people. Three years have passed since I became a parent yet I was struggling with a simple verse. "Unless the Lord builds the house, the builders labor in vain. Unless the Lord watches over the city, the guards stand watch in vain."

Jekalyn Carr sings the song Greater is Coming and she starts it by stating the following:

An olive has to go through three stages, for its oil to run: It has to go through the shaking, the beating, and the pressing And just like the olive, some of you may have felt like you go through the shaking, the beating and the pressing. You've went through all of that for your oil to flow Now, your greater is coming...

The words of this song have ministered in such a great way as I journey through this groundbreaking of my life. The clarity is simply that if I want to become a conveyer of the anointing, if I want to be the vessel though which the oil of the almighty will flow then I must go through the "shaking, the beating, and the pressing." Wow! Jesus said to Peter, "Simon, Simon, Satan has asked for you to sift you (shake you) as wheat but I have prayed for you and when you are strong, strengthen your brothers." If ever you or I want to be able to strengthen our brothers, our neighbor, our friend, we will have to allow God to take us through this process. **The trials will not be because Satan has**

won but because God has a plan. Jesus has already prayed us through. All we have to do is stand in the midst of the storm.

As I wrote this book, the Lord revealed to me the value of tools used in the ground breaking. I preached a sermon, "Don't resent the tools". I shared that

"As God gets ready to shift you into your purpose, position you for your destiny let your focus not be on Tyre (those who are laughing at you, talking bad about you, hating on you) and others but rather consider the tools that God has sent and allow him to finish the work he started." What I could see more clearly is that we are easily distracted by what is. God allowed me to understand the obvious, in a groundbreaking; losing sight of the destiny before us, Peter does not have control of the tools. Have you ever seen the ground reach up and hold on to the tools? Have you ever seen the ground guide the tool, telling it where to hit, how hard to hit, what to hit and what not to hit? "It is not to see how much you can endure before you say no more. The ground breaking is done by the construction worker/builder". If God is to work on us and fulfill his plan in us, we have to take our hands off of the tools.

Except the Lord builds he must first break ground. The ground is indicative of your existence, your ego, and your pride. The ground is indicative of your health, family, and ministry. You don't determine, I do not determine the ground but if God is going to work in each of us, he has to break up what has the potential of creating a coronary attack in our growth so that he can expose it and eradicate it.

God is so awesome that in the process of writing this book, there was work to be done outside of my home where the city had to open up the sidewalk in front of my house in order to reroute a pipe. I watched as they broke ground, removed the large pieces of concrete in order to expose the dirt. The work was not then complete, it was only beginning. One would think that with exposed concrete they would now be able to clear the dirt and begin rerouting the pipe. The more dirt they removed the more the trunk of the old tree that was there was exposed. With the concrete on top of it, there was a noticeable rise but it was not a problem. But once it was exposed, it became a problem. The workers could not complete their work until the old trunk and all of its roots were removed.

They spent more time working on all sides of the old trunk until finally they could remove the trunk, the roots and everything around it. The Lord showed me that when he breaks ground in our lives it is a process. There will be times where an old trunk with roots in our lives will be exposed and the only way he can continue is by removing it. It will hurt, we will suffer a while but after that we will find joy and peace. One of my mentors once shared with me, when God takes his broom and sweeps things out the door do not go back and pick it up. As I watched the process, it was clear in my spirit, when God starts to move people or fixtures from your life, what he sweeps out don't try to pick up again. This is where we walk with the writer of Hebrews that says,

> *"What is faith? It is the confident assurance that what we hope for is going to happen. It is the evidence of things we cannot yet see." Hebrews 11:1*

As a child of God who wants to walk in his plan for our lives, we have to get to a place of surrender where we say okay, Lord, you are the builder. I am hurting, it's difficult but I trust you. I trust you even when the pain is too hard to utter the word trust, I still trust you. It became clearer to me that what makes the process so painful is that when your hands are off you have no control. This is not good for control freaks. People who can't release or let go can never get to where God fully wants to take them because they are too busy being God. If God is the builder then he will determine the location, where he wants you to work, live and minister. He has already established your position; in fact it was established before you were. Before the foundation of this world, like Jeremiah, God knew you and he established you. If we grasp that then we can become more receptive to the intensity of the blow, the depth of the digging to then appreciate the height of his positioning in us. He has established the total plan for our lives. Will we trust him enough? If he doesn't build, all we do will be in vain.

God showed me how the workers used the tools; a saw, a shovel, a machine used like an axe to break up the slabs of concrete, and another I couldn't identify. The tools, however, drew me to the reference I used in my message: the pickaxe, the shovel, the hoe, and the pitchfork. Each instrument serves a purpose.

The pickaxe to break ground and pull up the slab of concrete it is breaking. It is the first blow so it is the most painful, the blow that comes unexpected. It is sharp and direct. It is a blow that severs ties instantly. It's the story of best friends who have lived a life since little girls doing everything together until tragedy hits, terminal illness. One friend sits holding the hand of her lifelong friend as she gradually leaves this world. Or it is the blow of one day you are holding on to your husband and because of a misunderstanding, he is ripped from your side. He is incarcerated and then deported, gone for 11 years and finally pardoned to return freely to the USA, as was the real story of one of my pastors. The blow could be tragic physically or mentally. It could be the first time someone insults your appearance, you are called half-human, and something that never left your thoughts. For years you believe you are until you realize things said in anger are not always applicable but the blow of it if you are not careful can damage a persons image. The blow of the pickaxe separates what was. You are thrust into a new norm that takes shape not instantly but over a period of time. That's where God comes in, will you allow him to continue the work he has begun or take over from here. Will it be like the person saying, thanks, I can take over from here?

I mentioned before that I was in a womb for 5 ½ years and it is now that I understand why some of the things that were happening around me took place. Those serve purpose for another book.
What I do want to focus on is two times most recently that

the axe fell on me like a thunderbolt. The first is when I realized my daughter was no longer a teenager. She was in a place of self-discovery and I could no longer help her, rescue her like I would like to. I felt I had failed her. I was supposed to take care of her and I did not, or so I thought. *I had put her in a box of perfect protection.* I knew her earlier years were filled with trials so I became her refuge, her Rahab. I didn't know that the physical protection would have slipped out of my hands so quickly. I didn't know who to talk to but God. For so long I struggled wanting to save, wanting to protect someone who didn't know how to shake the past to embrace the future. I questioned myself as a pastor. How could I counsel families about putting God in the center when my house was where it was, or so I thought? I prayed, we prayed. There was love in the home. It was never a question of who was center of my life, our lives. The challenge was that we were at different places in our walk and I was impatient with the process.

God showed me, and it took a while that I was full of pride and ego. I was more concerned about what the world would think about my family and me that I lost sight of what was important. When the focus shifts from what others will think and not what God thought he ceased from building the house. I learned through that one verse that the understanding of God building the house meant He had to be the builder. He had to be the designer. He had to be the one to determine the finished product. How dare me and how dare anyone try to put a boxed in definition of what that looks like. My nutcracker is far from perfect but it is in her imperfection that God is molding her into her destiny. There were times I was so terrified of her decisions that I became one of those parents asking God to do some interesting things just so I could see her walk through the door. God taught me and is teaching me that the paradigm cannot shift if there is not one to shift in who she is to become.

The axe severed who I was and the attitude I had toward what being a parent and a pastor should look like. It severed the understandings I had of what the family should look like as I was raised.

I understood I had to get to a place of loving my parents

for their excellent parenting. They did an excellent job on us. But my nutcracker and anyone God gives me to parent will need the paradigm that He has established for them. The church will not determine what that will look like. I sing the song, "Lord I want to be just like you because she wants to be like me." In her own way, I see her looking more like me, did I mention she is Puerto Rican. I have a dear friend whom I would call "firecracker" she is also Puerto Rican and when she gets challenged its the Fourth of July. So now you understand why I mention that from time to time about my nutcracker. My comment is from experience and not discriminatory in any way as I distinguish between the cultures you study and the culture you interact with on a day-to-day basis. Don't get it twisted.

The second blow I would like to mention is September 22, 2014. On the 22nd of September I attended a meeting where clarity was brought to my call. My time had expired at the Lawrence Evangelical Church (LEC). I left with such a weight lifted. The Lord had already prepared me in such a way that I felt like that day positioned me on a catapult. It was pulled back and I was launched into my full purpose. It was a blow that was sudden, timely and perfect. Prior to the blow, I remember one day speaking with my nephew. Wow! I now understand why God sent him here. I remember when he attended the Pastors and Leaders Conference in Orlando, FL. It was after his graduation. He had decided he would stay in FL and work with by brother. But the Lord spoke to him and quickly following the conference he was with me in Massachusetts. The transition has not been easy but it is all making sense now. I remember sitting in my car with him a week prior and just expressing to him how exhausted I was and hoping for something new. He did what he normally did because he knew I didn't talk much so when I did, I needed just an ear. I had no idea I was speaking into my future. Someone described it as the chains were broken, the rocks rolled away and now I am going to run. I am experiencing what the writer meant in Hebrews 12:1-2 NKV

> *"Wherefore seeing we also are compassed about with so great a cloud of witnesses, let us lay aside every weight, and the sin which doth so easily beset us, and let us run with patience the race that is set before us, ²Looking unto Jesus the author and finisher of our faith; who for the joy that was set before him endured the cross, despising the shame, and is set down at the right hand of the throne of God."*

There was the pain of the blow, which I will not deny. I am a very stable person so I do not like shifting. I like to be still for as long as I can and some times it can be at a fault. Nonetheless, that separation was difficult but necessary. In order for a tree to grow, regardless of how you might try to understand or justify it, pruning is necessary from time to time. Not every match is a perfect match. God has us in places for a season and when it is time to move, he makes the environment uncomfortable to where you can no longer find peace. I knew God had called me. I was in total peace. I just did not know that I was the slab of stone that was in the way that he had to break in order to get me where he wanted me. Sometimes we are the ones in the way and God has to use tools, people, situations or circumstances to get us to where he wants us.

There were moments in the two scenarios where I found myself before God not asking why but asking how. **I learned long ago that God is God and when he begins to do something we need to let him.** I confess I was often in the way and sometimes I didn't realize it. The situation with my nutcracker and my shift from LEC pushed me into a new strength with God. As I watched the men who were working outside of my house, I watched as they removed rocks and continued digging. They worked between the shovel and other tools. They used the shovel to remove the rocks to then begin the next phase, which would require the hoe and the pitchfork. Once the rocks were removed, they started moving the dirt on the surface. The further down they went the more complicated it became. They came in contact with the roots of the old tree that was once there. For a long time I watched as they worked to remove the roots.

They worked even harder as they dug up the small roots but had to bring in more tools, a saw to help cut away and dig out the trunk. As I looked it was as though God was saying there would be times in our lives where the nature of the project will require me to go deeper. I will come across the roots of old trees, old wounds, old hurts and the purpose will not be to remind you of them but relieve you of them because I am about to do a new thing.

Some of my earlier ramblings about things that took place in my infancy surfaced as my nutcracker was going through her period of self-discovery. I understand why it was so important for me to take care of her, protecting her from a big bad world. Who was I fooling? I had the best protection as a child and the big bad world still found me, and I had both parents. There is no perfect home, no perfect family unless there be a perfect presence of the builder. I now see the shield had broken and the dirt was uncovering, exposing roots that needed to be shared so that others can be healed. They needed to be exposed so that the flow that was upon me could freely flow in me. The pain of the past has been cut down like that old tree but the next thing that God needed to do was to remove the trunk. Based how deep the roots are, he will determine how long he will need to spend on this next phase of the ground breaking. Regardless the pastor, leader, CEO, it does not matter.

You will not be effective and whole until you come to terms with the hidden roots that stand in the way of you and the purpose of your true existence. A rich man would not be miserable if he was not constantly dealing with the hidden. A poor man would not be miserable if he was not constantly dealing with the hidden. **There is a pain to be rich and a pain to be poor.** However, if the chief architect, the builder and sustainer of our joy were allowed to handle the tools, rich or poor we can have peace. I understood from God that as he unearthed the roots, he needed to clear all obstruction so that my river can flow. He needed to clear all obstruction so that my purpose could grow.

As I drove away from the church, I watched as God began using a spiritual shovel to lift things and people out of my life. He was swift. He was intentional. He was strategic. He was public. It was the best pain I could have ever experienced. I love the body and continue to do so. I went home and saw how within 24 hours I had greater purpose. God had begun the work he had promised a while ago. A church had been formed. I remember my nephew again, God I love him. We were back and forth texting ideas of a new church and what the name of it would be. I shared the name with a few others and in no time we had it. Flowing Rivers International Church. Ezekiel 47:8 *"Then said he unto me, These waters issue out toward the east country, and go down into the desert, and go into the sea: which being brought forth into the sea, the waters shall be healed."* God had birthed a mouthpiece for the nations. It would bring forth words of healing and hope. Everywhere we would go, we would bring forth life. New England was coming to Jesus. All of us could feel it, could experience it, and could understand that what was happening in our midst was supernatural.

The old me, would probably have taken a little longer to get going, spending time trying to make sense of things. But God had me in a womb for 5 ½ years. I was being groomed for such a time as this. The ground breaking was to birth out a Pastor. It was to birth out a church. 7 years ago I would not have been able to tell you I had a pastor or a church in me. But I now understand why God told me the first time I preached at an open-air service in Lowell. We were in a park and on my way there God told me to preach to the masses. There may have been 50 people in the park but he told me to preach as though I was standing before a multitude.

When your ground breaks, do not believe it to be without purpose. If we really want God to work in us, we have to allow him free reign in our lives to break when he wants, to lift debris when he wants and to remove even the things we love the most even if it hurts. Trust me, there is no greater glory than serving God. If he removes something or someone from our lives it's because he has a greater plan and they had become like the tree trunk and the old roots that needed to be eradicated so that a new oil can flow. The word of God says you can't put new wine in old wineskin. We can't put new anointing in a vessel that cannot contain it. The anointing that is to flow on nutcracker requires that she does not take on my skin but step into her own. It is a challenge to watch the process but my spiritual eyes are watching God at work. Praise God!

Rest in the Promise

> Hebrews 4:3-4 *"For we which have believed do enter into rest, as he said, As I have sworn in my wrath, if they shall enter into my rest: although the works were finished from the foundation of the world. ⁴ For he spake in a certain place of the seventh day on this wise, And God did rest the seventh day from all his works."*

When we believe in the word of God we see that in our obedience to Him as he promised Israel so he promises us and that is a place of rest. This is a place that was established from the foundation of the world. In other words, we are guaranteed rest in God. V4 speaks to when God rested on the seventh day. It was not because of exhaustion but because the work was complete. That tells us today that His promises, which are yes and amen, mean we do not have to worry about anything. Just trust Him and take Him at His word. That being said, it would make sense that we release the tools and allow him to complete his purpose in our lives.

Days have past and the work outside of my house is still incomplete. The workmen completed the most integral part, the pipe is in and the street portion sealed. However, the area where the trunk was with all the old roots remains unfinished. They put down new dirt and left it there. The impact was so great that they need to give the new dirt time to settle into its new environment. I would imagine they also put down some chemicals to prevent the roots from returning. **Sometimes we are in a hurry to cover up the pain.** We are in such a hurry to cover up the blow. God was teaching me through the work being done outside my home that when he is done digging, when he is done removing the hindrances, he has to give it some time for you to get used to your new environment before he can begin building. He will not lay the new foundation on unstable ground. If he puts it down two quickly we might try to make it look like the last situation we came out of. God showed me that what he was doing in my life, I would become a designers original, no copycats. I learned that the Juliet Rose took 15 years before it reached perfection. 15 years, £13,000 or almost $5 million later it was the most expensive rose to produce. God revealed what he was doing with me through this process would not be a replica but an original. We try; I have tried to hurry God in the process when what he wanted me to do was rest. I wont say I have perfected what that looks like. However, I know more now and I do have greater clarity on trusting God in all things. Some people become pledged to man and relationships so much so that in the face of great difficulties when a choice is to be made they cling to the familiar. Unfortunately we are living in a day where choosing God is increasingly more unpopular. The rest promised to us has no room for associations or familiar but a faith in a promise. It is finished so I don't need to fight. He is Jehovah Jirreh, my provider, so I don't need to worry. He is Jehovah Nissi, the one who reigns in victory, so my battles are won. He is Jehovah Shama, God who is present, so in my yesterday, today and tomorrow he is eternally present.

One of the greatest challenges yet requirements is sincerely pausing and resting. I grew up watching very active parents. They still are. We could not stay in the bed past am. I would say the four of us children learned from our parents not to sit idly by. There was always work to be done. The bed that looks so attractive to lie in is like a bed of thorns after a few hours of rest. I do not recommend that to anyone because I am now teaching myself to appreciate a couple more hours. I mean it's actually okay to sleep to 8 am sometimes. Glory to God! This is not the type of resting that I am referring to however. I am referring to a rest were we can stand on a bridge with the bungee cord of faith wrapped around our ankles and we simply release. We hold our arms out, close our eyes and say, "Lord here I come. I can't see you but I know you are there." I can't see the wind but I know it is there.

Noah didn't see the flood but he trusted you enough to build an ark only based on your word. The Hebrew Boys had not seen you but they trusted you enough to know that you were a jealous God and you commanded that they should not have other Gods but you. They did so to the extent that they walked into a fiery furnace and walked out untouched. It was not who they were but their faith in knowing who you were. **This resting is seeing the fire and moving forward.**

Lets get personal for a moment. This journey that I am now on is awesome and scary. I am in a place I have never been. This place may resonate with the parent who has lost a child, the athlete who had big dreams cut short by a sudden injury, the CEO who one day you are in the corner office and the next day you are walking out a "failure". I don't know where you are at this moment in your life but that place feels dark, alone, consuming, overpowering, stifling and hopeless. It is not a happy place but a necessary place. Weird as it may seem because of the loss of a child a lot of foundations have been established to help other parents with their children. Because of that injury you did not go pro but you are helping countless others reach their dream. Because you were denied the corner office you now own the company. All of this comes from that place you had never been. I have been in the giving and receiving end of "that place"; have you? The funny thing is a lot of people remain in that place not knowing that in the midst of all of that they can find peace. In the midst of all challenges described they can find joy and rest. You can't see your way clear but you can trust the way maker.

All I know is I love God and trust him enough not to limit him. I do not have much. I do not have many in my intimate circle. I am holding on 100% not based on what or whom I know on earth but on God and his word. I am literally saying to you my readers; this resting place requires a lot of work. The work is not physical but spiritual. I have been put under the axe of life. The dirt of me has been exposed. Roots have been plucked out. I have some new dirt that has been poured in to the fill the vacancy. My faith has never been more challenged. You can tell a person's faith level by their reaction in the midst of a storm. It is like boiling water the hotter the water gets, the least likely we are to dip our fingers. I remember being in the hot springs in Costa Rica. We were at the base of the volcano and in each natural spring, the closer you get to the volcano the hotter the water. Not many people went that close. The same was the test of my faith. I spoke about it, I preached about it but now that I was in the furnace, was I going to live it? Was I going to trust the God I knew or the emotions that consumed me? My love for God has never felt more real. My trust in his word and his promises is all that I have. I am anchored in him and all of who he is. This is not easy to say when Sunday after Sunday I stand to deliver the word God has given me for his people. The shift I must say in my messages is that they are now more real. They are not preaching in abstraction. I find that in this place of groundbreaking and in this season of rest, God is putting me on a next level platform.

I am watching God build two houses. He is building my household and me. He is also building his church. God is the visible chief architect and builder. It is about him guiding us through the building process.

In my life, I have never been this focused and responsible. I am more accountable with everything. It is funny, we sit on a chair because it is there and looks like it will hold us up. Some times I don't think twice. The journey I am now on does not have physical chairs to sit on. There is not a steady paycheck. I have a house with a mortgage, a daughter in school, a car note, and bills. The highest weekly check I have received since my ground was split open was $600 and the lowest was $291. I came from a secular background of making over $100k a year. Yes friends, God has begun a good work in me. I am trusting if he feeds the birds in the air, the fish in the sea and the animals in the forest then he will feed me. He will supply. I trust God! I should be losing my mind but I am not, God has become my chair, my strength, my hope, my all in all. I remember constantly telling God that I just wanted to focus on him and do the things that would glorify him.

Well, I got it! I am thankful. The bottom-line for me and prayerfully for all of you who want to "arrive" learn to let God build. ***In my little I have more than when I had more.*** God is awesome!

In the church, we have now completed eight weeks of worship as a newly formed church. Our first Sunday we had 52 people and the numbers last Sunday, week eight was approximately 150. These numbers include a children ministry that was active since the first day. As he sends them, I am seeing how through the sermons God is challenging those who started with me and those who he is sending. I see how easy it is for young (as defined by experience and maturity in the word) preachers, pastors to get carried away in the pulpit. I always get nervous when I see people anxious to get to a position. They will do all they can to get there, impatiently trying to take over and jump into the glimpse of what God may or may not have shown them. Not because someone prayed over you means you need to run into action. Before I became a Pastor, I now reflect on how long God has been grooming me for now. I was not cooked in the microwave. All my life I have had struggles and blessings. I didn't understand the end but God had it expected, predetermined. I never dreamt of becoming a pastor. I knew I was called to ministry, and acknowledged in my early 20s that I was called to serve. I would never have been able to say it was to become a pastor let alone the founder of a church. The only thing that has been constant in my life is how much I love God and want to live for him. In my imperfection I want to be perfected in him.

ARTIFACT #3

Before the Build

Have you ever found yourself feeling exposed? It's that feeling of nowhere to run, nowhere to hide; you are wide open. Everyone that is looking at you can read right through you. Even if they can't, you feel like they can. I think, now I know that one of the reasons why so many people, myself included have such a difficult time being real with ourselves and as a pastor with our congregation is that we are afraid of being exposed. I remember in college one of the stories that we read was on the "El Que Diran" or "what will they say". It is the constant preoccupation of what others would say.

I realize as I am at this place of vulnerability and strength in my life that my years of insecurity and low self-esteem are finally nearing an end. I say nearing not because I am not delivered but rather because I am delivered and when the enemy places thoughts in my head I know I need to remind him it is over. It is finished. Just by looking at me, one would not know that I grew up with extremely low self-esteem. I was very quiet, very reserved, and doubted my every step. I considered myself to be the ugliest or among the ugliest alive. Well, when you are called ugly and made to feel ugly for so long you believe it. My family loved me but society had other opinions. Let's face it. I was a rather large kid in middle school and high school. I was the least likely to do or become anything in all categories. I should not have accomplished what I did. The test scores said I would not go far, I sure proved them wrong. I now know enough to say to God be the Glory.

This feeling of being exposed is one that at another point in my life I may have run and hid. I appreciate that God has brought me to this place where the surface that once covered me is now removed and I am truly wide open. I am a pastor, but in essence I am unemployed, receiving an offering based on the weekly blessing. I work for the State but that is a contracted position and the compensation will not come until the contracts have ended and the books close 42 days later. The bills are piling up. The mortgage is over due and saving the house will be on a prayer, a miracle from God. I have a daughter in school. It's the holiday season. I have several major projects all of which need time, prayer, and resources. My health is at an all time low. I am wide open.

I find myself at the greatest crossroads of life and contrary to who I used to be. I find that I have inner peace that keeps me calm and more driven than ever. There is a calm that I have in my spirit that it is well. For with the righteous, it shall be well. I believe it.

In this period of exposure, I am realizing the impact it is having on my intimacy with God, my parenting, my preaching, my finances, and my relationships.

Intimacy with God

I have become an emotional wreck. I find myself really crying out to God more than I have ever done before. I am at such a level of hunger and thirst for him. On Thanksgiving Day, I did something I had never before done, at least not like this. I called my parents and said we are going to pray and give thanks. God used us in such a powerful way. We prayed, we gave thanks and made declarations that were so powerful. Those prayer warriors know what I am talking about where when you come out of a prayer so deep you feel like you could conquer the world. I am finding now that I am exposed and that my only covering is God. He is the blanket that shields my nakedness.

As pastors and leaders, I find that we teach and emphasize the importance of developing an intimate relationship with God. We tell people the right thing, what the word of God says about seeking him and being hungry for him. We teach people that the best hiding place is in the shelter of His wings. We teach and preach so much and ironically, at least in my case, when the tables are turned though we say the same to ourselves we buckle under the weight of the pressure. The truth and depth with which we can really measure the extent to which God has become our builder and the foundation secure is when we are under our own pressure. We are the pastors, we are the mentors so who do we turn to? This journey brought me back to the moments I cried out in the shower, telling God, ***"If you called me you have to mentor me."*** Now I see myself more than ever going back to those moments and telling God, "I have no where to go. You have me. What do you want me to do? Show me what to do." So many times, that was my cry to Him. I would tell him, "Lord, dad, can you just hold me?" I would literally sit there on the floor with my head on the bed as though placed on the lap of my father.

My Parenting

One of my challenges is to see the process my nutcracker is going through and wanting to rescue her. Paul says in 1 Corinthians 3:6, "My job was to plant the seed in your hearts, and Apollos watered it, but it was God, not we, who made it grow." This scripture has become the sedative to my emotional rollercoaster. I know she belongs to God and these are trying years for her. I also know that God has His hands on her. It is not for me to try and perfect what is already perfect. God has her right where He wants her and at His perfect time, she will reflect His glory. This was an important moment for me because as a parent, as a pastor, as a single pastor parent, it is easy to stress about the view of the onlooker. As I mentioned earlier, this journey is one that only God can determine. Being exposed allows me to be real from the pulpit, in my book and in moments of mentoring with other families who are struggling. It IS God who does the breaking and the building.

I remember one night I cried out to God, trying to understanding the growing pains of parenting an adult and God placed in my spirit the following: *"your job is to love her, my job is to correct her."* That came home so clear to me that from that moment on, it has not been perfect, but I have really released the things I cannot change into His hands. As a pastor and as a parent, this is a difficult thing to do. However, if God allows the exposure it is for no other reason than to position us for His purpose. It is now, in the release, that He will really be able to build the relationship that He designed us to have. It is now that God will be glorified in our relationship He makes the seed grow, not me. Praise God for exposure!

My Preaching

I recommend this to every pastor or anyone desirous of becoming a public figure. Although, I must stress my emphasis is on those who profess to wanting to be real with those God has placed under their care. I preached my heart out for 5 ½ years to a body of believers who I loved and thank God for the time I served them. However, I did not feel then like I feel now. As I mentioned before, thank you September 22, 2014. I feel like that old movie The Twilight Zone. I feel like I stepped out of one era into another. My preaching is like night and day. I feel like I have come alive in a way I did not know existed. I still can never tell you all of what I said. I do know that the spirit of the Lord is moving mightily and lives are being transformed. The writing of this book is taking place as the transition is occurring so I also am preaching my journey. **Pastors, preach your journey!** The Word is what makes the shift. The Word is that agent that brings Rema to a simple message. The anointing is more real because it is connected to the person God has established you to be. I am exposed not for internment but for revelation. The curtains come off; the mask is lifted when you are exposed. The nakedness of the passion for Christ shifts from what you read and study to who you are.

My Finances

Once my dad reads this book he will probably smile from ear to ear to learn that finally I got it. He would hammer us, as we got older to save. "You need to save, you need to have something put away for a rainy day." Well, my rainy day was my parents following a long lecture from him. I knew he was right but never took it as serious as I should. I had the accounts but the money entered and left, quickly. Have a budget and follow it. Well, I could follow a budget that was pre-established but my skill was not to prepare my own budget. Bottom-line, I needed help. I didn't ask for help. How could I? I had four degrees and a couple of certificates under my belt. I made good money, why would I ask for help? Well this was the area where I needed God the most. I did a poor job balancing my books. I did a poor job saving and leaving it there. There was always a need to dip. I was also terrible whenever there was a need. I was one of those people who would give everything away and keep nothing for myself. Yes, I was being kind but it was not what God meant in being a good steward.

I didn't play with giving in church. I love giving to God. I believe in giving. I knew what to do but I did not apply it to my person and God used this season to order my financial steps. I say He is positioning me to receive what is to come. Praise God He knows he can trust me to bless others, to give in Church and to not idolize the mighty dollar. I remember I would cry out to God and tell Him, enough, I need to change. I need to have something to show for my hard work. God answered. In my exposure, I have built a personal budget and am sticking to it. I have built other budgets and am sticking to them. There are appropriate allocations that make sense. No one taught me this when I started but God. If God is going to take me to this next place that I see in the spirit realm then this was necessary.

If God is to build my house, He is showing me what He needed me to see by way of my responsible stewardship. If He is going to use me to preach on stewardship, I need to have a testimony. I have so many eyes looking at me and too many that God has placed in my care for me to lead. This exposure though painful was necessary.

My Relationships

One of the most insecure times for me was the 5½ years of pastoring in the area of relationships. This is not to be misunderstood as I had an experience I would not change and met some remarkable people who have impacted my life forever. Bishop TD Jakes said it best. It is difficult for a young pastor to go into a pre-established church and try to lead it. In one sermon, talking to pastors and leaders, he highlights the reality that Jesus knew his Judas. He also knew his Peter. The challenge was not, however on the one who would betray Jesus but on the 11 who asked the question, "Lord is it I?" That message resonated with me for so long because in a new environment where you inherit everyone, you do not know. The variables are many. Who do you trust? Who is actually with you? Who will be your Confidants, the ones you can count on thick or thin? They are there for you regardless. Who will be your Constituents, the ones who will walk with you until another opportunity arises to get them to their destination faster than you? These are people who are not for you but they are with you for the ride. Who will be the Comrades, only there because you have a common enemy? Well I didn't have any common enemies when I started except Satan. I sincerely struggled being the outsider, knowing no one and trying to do the best I knew with what I had. There were those who said I love you but only God knows. **I was exposed not so that I could go into silence or hiding but so that I could stand on a mountaintop.** I will only say that I love the power of the experience and the purpose of the exposure. Many are watching to see if I will stop but the truth is simple, when God is leading he renews your strength every step of the way. This exposure has allowed me to see the truth of the "I love you." It is awesome!

I remember having two "armor bearers" on either side of me. It was quite the experience. I learned a lot about what I want and do not want. I learned about who was there to support and who was not. I learned so much that it is with gratitude that I acknowledge the experience. The day came where I found myself sitting alone. The covering that I had for several months in the blink of an eye was no longer there. There is so much that could be said here but it would not do justice to the value of the experience. As God exposed me, He reminded me of my reliance. It must be totally on Him and never on man. **You see, when the physical person who is pledged to be by your side disappears, God will stand firm.** Where would I be today if I still relied on man? My call and strength was never on man and God had to interrupt the flow to remind me. It is good to have them but they are not your strength. When God is building, He must be the column. More on the column later.

This exposure brought revelation to me on who I could count on. They were people who were willing to stand in the midst of the storm with me, not because of me but because of the God in me. It was clear to them and to me that God had knitted our spirits together in such a way, words cannot explain. Let's put it this way. Our first Sunday, we had 52 people in attendance. Among them two pastors, a worship team, leaders in ministry and others who simply wanted to worship where we were. We opened our first day with a Children Church that continues to average 20-25 every Sunday. I could list all of what God has done in a short while but the purpose is simply to highlight that this exposure birthed a family.

The love and support that I have received since starting the church keeps me increasingly more humbled before God. It is now that I am nervous. This call is not to be taken lightly and I am finding that this exposure has given me greater accountability for service in the kingdom. I have great clarity in the call. I have a profound appreciation for the impact it is having on my intimacy with God, my parenting, my preaching, my finances, and my relationships.

ARTIFACT #4

Thoughts from a message: "I've been exposed – who am I?"

We completed four weeks on Groundbreaking and how not to resent the tools God uses in our lives to take us into our purpose. It was time to move on to the foundation and the construction, or so I thought. God would use my personal situations as mentioned above to reveal to me some truths.

The first truth was that not because the ground is broken means we should start building right away. He revealed it is a process and while the ground was now open, he had some damage control to do so that there would not be any hemorrhaging once the foundation is laid. I think about a dentist. When you go to get a root canal done, they numb your gums, drill into the tooth, take out all of the roots and put in temporary filings with medication. The goal is that when they seal up the tooth at a later visit, there would not be susceptibility to infection. It also allowed the dentist to see that in fact all roots were removed. I remember once that was done. I was attending the University of Illinois at Urbana Champaign. I had a root canal done and needed to return the following week. Well, I returned and sat in the dentist chair for what was supposed to be a normal procedure. To my pain and the dentist's dismay, I jumped out of the seat at the first contact with my tooth. He had not thoroughly removed the roots.

I have had many root canal experiences in my journey where the pinch of the pain takes me back to that point of origin. Christmas with the family, though simple was an extraction for me. I explain. My parents instilled in us not only the value of family but also family traditions. We had Sunday dinners. We had family meetings. Christmas gatherings were something we all looked forward to, and then we grew up. All of my siblings got married established a family and one year decided it was time to start their own traditions. They wanted to stay in their own homes. I was like, what? What about me? I am single. I don't have my own family and you guys are my family. It was an extraction that hurt. The saying time heals all wounds is not true. Every year I still long for the family time I grew up knowing. Time has changed, we have changed, but the value remains. This was one of those moments where, when I reflect on the emotional state I was in and all the insecurities I was living through it was another moment of rejection. I didn't realize it until later. I never mentioned it until now, but I felt like my world was caving in and there was nothing I could do. As I mention it from time to time, it is as though a wound was being tugged at. No, I love my siblings and they love me so I have no inner family fights with them to share with the world. I do know that as God is building my house, he is bringing to light some areas in my life that now open can be released.

I have since had my own established traditions and our families have moments of celebration but there is nothing like being with mom and dad and the rest of the family at Christmas.

Another truth about the groundbreaking was that now that I was wide open, exposed, as mentioned before, there were some areas that needed to be addressed prior to entering into the next phase of my life. In 2 Corinthians 3:18 Paul hits the nail right on the head.

"And all of us have had that veil removed so that we can be mirrors that brightly reflect the glory of the Lord. And as the Spirit of The

Lord works within us, we become more and more like him and reflect his glory even more."

While this text speaks of the salvation that is freely given to all who come to Jesus and the veil that is taken away, it shines brightly on the groundbreaking experience.

If we consider a definition of the word exposure, we understand that what was once covering us is now gone. We are left wide open. If we were once shielded, covered or protected, we are now visible to the naked eye. Mama was no longer there; daddy was no longer there. There was no one to fight the battles or no one to protect you are exposed. The veil has been lifted, the curtains drawn, your ugly is out, you have been exposed. You are at a place of vulnerability, susceptible to any and everything around.

One of the things I have come to appreciate is once I am done preaching, there are people around to pray over me and protect me from spiritual elements that can catch me off guard because I am drained. When I preach, everything that is in me is poured out and so there is nothing left to hold me up. Sometimes, literally I feel like I am going to connect with the floor if someone does not catch me. I mentioned the covering before but to God be the glory, as He is taking me on this journey I now see in this season of exposure that he had to remove in order to establish. He had to remove the scaffold that was temporary to put fixtures that would be permanent. Man could not do what God can. Man cannot build the house without the blueprints of God. This season of being unveiled has brought clarity to help the weak know that yes you are strong but your strength lies within. Position does not make us strong. Title does not make us strong. A bench does not make us strong, but it is the strength of God, the backbone of our purpose. God could not build this house; he cannot build your house unless he is able to eradicate false understandings. He cannot build your house unless he is able to lay a firm foundation. He cannot build a firm foundation on tainted soil.

God told Moses to take the shoes from off of his feet because the place he was standing was holy. He told Joshua to take off his shoes because he was on holy ground. The house that God builds in us will require the shoes of our false pretense, the shoes of our imaginary me, the shoes of our traditions and rituals that have nothing to do with the God that we serve be removed. I want God to build my house. I want to know that who I am to become in him is fully expressed in who he created me to be. I am not referring to the physical me that will just wither away with time. I am talking about the eternal me caught in the physical me placed here on earth for a purpose. This time of being wide open helped me to value who I am as a human and who I am as man, spirit.

Let me explain briefly, the word human comes from humus, which means dirt, and man, which is spirit. When God said in Genesis 1:26, "Then God said, "Let Us **make** man in **Our image**, according to **Our likeness**; let them have dominion over the fish of the sea, over the birds of the air, and over the cattle, over all the earth and over every creeping thing that creeps on the earth." He made man, according to their image and likeness. So if God is spirit, then man is spirit. Man then was created to live eternal after the likeness of God. He then took dirt and formed the body in which he blew his spirit and the dirt became a living thing. When I think about the exposure and being wide open before God can lay the foundation over my life, I am realizing that those things that are being exposed are being squeezed out because they cannot go with me to the place God is taking me. Formed means to squeeze. God is not going to squeeze neither the foundation nor the building. He broke me wide open to get rid of those hindrances and reveal those untapped strengths so that he can make the shift he already spoke over my life.

Don't run away from the breaking. Do not run away from the shifting of people, things or possessions out of your life. Do not run away from the exposure. You may, will hurt for a while.

Remember it is only a season, yes; the Greater is Coming, sing Ms. Jekalyn Carr. I am truly holding on to the lifeline and it is Jesus. I have not felt stronger, freer, or bolder. So look out world, here comes my healer, my redeemer, my way maker, my problem solver, and my el Shaddai. He is coming.

There is a freedom, ironically so, that comes with being exposed. I am learning that exposure does not have to cause pain if we understand the purpose. If I could sing and had a choir to back me up, I would sing this from every mountaintop, on every platform God allows. I worship God just because of who He is.

Lord I worship you by TS

Lord I worship you
Because of who you are//

You are my Lord
You are my King
You are the great I AM

Lord I worship you
Because of who you are//

You are my Lord
You are my King
You are the great I AM

You are my everything
You are my Lord and King
You are the great I AM
O Lord, my everything

Lord I worship you
Because of who you are//

You are my Lord
You are my King
You are the great I AM

I am, Jehova Rapha
I am, God your healer

I am, Jehova Nizzi
I am, I fight your battles

I am, Jehova Shama
I am, your God who's present

I am, Jehova Jirreh
I am, God your provider

Lord I worship you
Because of who you are//

You are my Lord
You area King
You are the great I am

I am, Jehova Rapha
I am, God your healer

I am, Jehova Nizzi
I am, I fight your battles

I am, Jehova Shama
I am, your God who's present

I am, Jehova Jirreh
I am, God your provider

Chorus

I believe there are people who have spent a lifetime undercover because they were once exposed and spent a lifetime trying to cover it up so their smile is not real, their strength is inflated, and they give people an impression of what/who they are not

To be exposed is not so that you can be humiliated. Exposure is an opportunity to see the source of our discontentment and guide us towards finding a responsible resolve. The thing that was once hidden in the darkness of the hard surface created by life has now been revealed. One of the things that I mentioned earlier is that we cannot be the ground and the tool at the same time. To reach the place God has laid before us, we need to release and faithfully rest in the peace of His presence. Exposure then will only happen when we allow the one holding the tools work his way to the source of the problem, even if it hurts.

I shared with the congregation that when we are exposed it is an opportunity to step into God's plan for our lives. The devil only has power over you when he can control your mind; keep you locked up in the fear of what if? You give away your personal power as a child of God when you fail to understand who you are and who is inside of you. You give away your personal power and live a life covered up, hiding behind the scar of the asphalt. You have built an empire to cover up your shame and insecurity. God is saying to us in our exposure that He is exposing us not so that we can be left wide open but so that we can begin to shine, reflecting the purpose of our creation

This journey has helped me to see and then share with others that the breaking of our ground serves the purpose as God shifts us to take us from where we are, from the hole you find ourselves in to the place God really intended for us to be. When God is the builder of our house let us give him permission to break the ground, lift the rocks and discard the weighty baggage that holds us down. From personal experience, it is a fact that true exposure lead to vulnerability but it also makes clear the path to our potential and purpose. This is the place where the answer begins to reveal itself of "who am I?" "What is my purpose?" This is the place where God speaks into our spirit to let us know the work he really wants to do in us requires a new foundation and if we are serious enough, the labor will not be in vain.

BUILDING AND SHAPING PHASE II

"I love you" An expression today that is overly used yet poorly understood. I remember growing up that this was not frequently stated. Oh my parents loved us and would do just about anything for us. They demonstrated their love for us primarily through acts. Don't get me wrong; we were not paid through allowances; get what we want if we cried or anything like that. It was the way they cared; the nurture they showed that caused us to know they loved us. However, for some reason I needed more. I needed to hear the words. I didn't say them but I needed to hear them. As a child growing up I didn't understand why it was important. Honestly, it is now after God is revealing to me the pain to my purpose that I get it. I get why if I was molested so early in life, having my parents tell me they loved me was important. I didn't get it then but I do now.

I remember the moment the ice broke, the shift occurred. I was not a little girl, I was now an adult and my mother took the first step. Her parents didn't say it to their children. In fact neither did my father. They were perpetuating what they grew up on. But one-day mamma decided she wanted her children to not just know but hear the words "I love you" loud and clear. I admit, it was awkward at first but over time I would look forward to talking with her because she always said, "I love you baby." My dad is now a seasonal guy in the "I love you" department but at least he dared to take the step of faith. Bless his heart.

I have to say; hearing those words unknowingly began a journey towards healing in me that I could not see before. Love was always there, not only my parents and family but also the love of God. I missed seeing this love thus craving it consequently left me in a place of longing. My ground breaking, my perfect storm helped draw me back towards a foundation I knew but overlooked.

Peace

Did you know that in order for the foundation to be laid and the construction to begin, the ground must reach a certain level of settling? Let me explain. As I watched the process of tearing up the ground, laying the pipes and prepping it to put down new concrete, there was a period of a few weeks where all the workers did was pour on dirt, pat it down and leave it so that it could settle. Once the dirt was settled and the ground was ready to be worked on, they returned to lay the concrete. This process prevents the early laying of concrete that would then give way because areas with air pockets were not worked out. As I pondered that process, God revealed to me the process we each go through or must go through as He builds our house.

> Philippians 4:6-7 says, *"Be anxious for nothing, but in everything by prayer and supplication, with thanksgiving, let your requests be made known to God; ⁷ and the peace of God, which surpasses all understanding, will guard your hearts and minds through Christ Jesus."*

One of the great life lessons I would share, as I understood what was transpiring outside and in my own personal life as well is that the foundation will not be laid and the construction will not begin until the air pockets have been pushed out. They will either be pushed out by force or by giving it time. Regardless how they are pushed out, the two opposing forces are at work, anxiety and peace, and we are the ones who have the power to determine who will win.

There were many times I found myself as woman, mother, and pastor, ready for God to build. I would say to him, here I am, build me or send me. In the midst of my attacks, in the midst of my trials, I would say send me. Do you know that God will not send you while you have air pockets? He is ready to build, anxious to do his work in your life and mine but he cannot, will not do what he wants until the pockets are pushed out. I know you are reading and saying, what? What is she talking about?

I wanted God to fix my situations, build my home so badly that I thought the best thing to do was to give Him a hand. Wrong! He did not need me as he formed me in my mother's womb and he definitely does not need me now. I thought that if God was building my home, then it had to look a certain way otherwise I would be judged. Funny, this is something I thought I had let go of before but as the little things in life become big things I realized more and more that pride was a huge issue for me as was control. I wanted to control what my home would look like because if I did then I would have the perfect pastor's home. My family, my daughter and I, would look and act the model way as examples for the world. Okay, big mistake. First, I did not know what the model way was supposed to look like. Second, the more I tried to become something for which I had no definition, the more hell broke loose in my home.

Let us consider this scenario, the ground that was covering me up all these years has been ripped open. I am now wide open, transparent to the onlooker. The one thing I have to hold on to that I thought would be private my family, is now being challenged. With the concrete over it before, the challenges were there but I was in a fatidic control mode. Now there is no concrete, my teenager is now an adult; I am expected to be an example to the congregation. I am expected to tell them what a godly home looks like. I am expected to pray healing over their families. No one was clued into the core of my pain. There were times where

I contemplated things that I dare not utter, not wanting to give them life. **My life, right before the foundation was to be laid became hell on earth.**

My dad would say the darkest point is right before dawn. I knew these were attacks of the enemy on my home, family, ministry, and life. I knew he was looking at how he could tear me down and drag me away. This was my moment where what Jesus said to Simon applied to me here. He said Satan had asked for him to sift him as wheat but that he had already prayed for him. This was my moment to hold on to the prayer of Jesus because no one else understood my pain like he did. No one understood my hurt like he did. I was locked away, living in a cave, surfacing to preach, teach, and eat. I zipped on a smile and unzipped it when I went home. I was supposed to be in the building process but instead I was in a colicky stage of preparation towards construction.

If you have ever had colic, it is a stage where you have such bad gas and every part of your body hurts. There is no relief of it, you literally feel like you are going to die. Though I have never had this experience, it is like passing stones for those who suffer from gallstones. It is a painful process.

This is a bittersweet place to be in because the pain is so great. It is a pain that is greater than having the old tree roots pulled out. It is a pain that is greater than being denied your innocence when you are a child and can do nothing about it. You do not know how to defend yourself and you are in pain. This pain is so great because you are literally looking at death, death of a relationship, which could be your family, your spouse, your children, your finance, your health or something that is dear to you in the face. You are staring it in the face and wanting to challenge it. You want to take the bull by the horn and say no. You will not destroy my marriage, my family, my health, my children, my finance, or whatever it is. You are strong. You are a fighter and you're saying no! You exercise your authority as a parent, as a spiritual leader or simply one who knows the word. You have been taught to do that and that is what you now teach. You are practicing your own teaching. What do you do when you do all the right logical things and nothing seems to work? How do you stand in the pulpit feeling defeated and acting strong?

My greatest pain was in not knowing how to rescue my daughter from her journey of discovery. My greatest pain was in not trusting God that although this journey was not what I would like for her it was one that I would not be able to fight for her, I was going to have to let go and let Him. **My greatest pain was in being so strong and being so weak.** I remember the long nights of tears and worry about her. I just wanted to go back to the days when she would leave her room, yes even at 19 and crawl into my bed and I would hold her as she slept. I wanted to protect her so badly I was protecting her from her. I trusted God but did I trust him enough to leave her to him? Do you trust God enough to leave your situation in His hands?

It was a Sunday evening; I had a long week of very little sleep due to the stresses of everything going on in my life. The quiet suppression of emotions poured out. it culminated in a Saturday night of tears for hours resulting in black and blue eyes. I had to wear make up to church the next day. Sunday came, I went, and God delivered His word. I was and remain just a vessel. Following service, I went to dinner with one of my former students. God set me up. He caused me to cry my last tear over my anxiety for my daughter the night before. Do you know Go will set you up? Never miss out on a divine appointment, it could change your life. God allowed me to have dinner with this young lady who shared her story to the extent that I had an epiphany, an eye opener to where my daughter was and what I needed to do. I felt the great pain that I was carrying for months lifted. I was able to understand the peace of God in my situation. I saw how God was about to build a non traditional house that may defy the reasoning of some as to what the home of a pastor should look like and connect with the real people who understand that you do not get to your purpose without first experiencing the pain. I would and will be able to minister not to the perfect people out there but to the people like me who have baggage but whose house God is building.

In all of this I discovered that in order for the construction to begin, there has to be a great degree of inner peace. I am not talking about the peace you wear in an outfit or behind expensive jewelry and makeup. I am not talking about the peace that a fancy meal could get you and then you stop eating. The peace I am referring to is the one mentioned in the text above from Philippians where anxiety is replaced with the type of peace that regulates our hearts and minds. I honestly did not know what that was until I had that conversation with my former student and then got up off of my knees from the most intense prayer a mother can have. I felt God minister to me saying, "your job is to love, and my job is to take care of her." It was so clear that I finally rested. The atmosphere in my home changed that moment. My perspective on life and our relationship took a 180 shift that day. In calmness and serenity I shared with her where I was and walked away. Where she thought I was going to be the heavy handed parent I had been in the past, she instead encountered a "Nina" that only wanted to love her.

For you my readers, I encourage you this, do not try to begin construction unless you have reached the level of peace I am describing. You would be building your house on quicksand and with the slightest of movement it will begin to sink. I confess, with all of my accolades, with all of my preparation and the countless people I have helped over the years, I have never found myself at this place where the peace is beyond me. There are so many more areas in my life that have been positively affected only because I took the chance to trust God truly in "everything". I'll talk more on reaching a level of peace in the Phase IV Lessons Learned.

The Underlying Rock

I preached a sermon once talking about the roots of the palm tree and the ginger root. I focused on the complexity of the roots in that their stability lie in the way they are anchored around underlying rocks. Palm trees for example are able to withstand the most brutal weather and remain standing. They sway and they bend but they rarely if ever fall. Their resistance is attributed to the support they have with the rock below. In Luke 7:46-49 NKJV Jesus says:

[46] *"But why do you call Me 'Lord, Lord,' and not do the things which I say?* [47] *Whoever comes to Me, and hears My sayings and does them, I will show you whom he is like:* [48] *He is like a man building a house, who dug deep and laid the foundation on the rock. And when the flood arose, the stream beat vehemently against that house, and could not shake it, for it was founded on the rock.* [49] *But he who heard and did nothing is like a man who built a house on the earth without a foundation, against which the stream beat vehemently; and immediately it fell. And the ruin of that house was great."*

As I purposed myself more in understanding the text of Psalm 127:1, the essence of this book, what Jesus is saying in Luke becomes clearer. We spend a lifetime at times trying to establish such a firm foundation. Our parents worked hard and so we work hard with a focus on leaving a legacy for their children, our children to follow. There is nothing wrong with that concept except when it is misplaced. **A misplaced understanding of building foundations can cause man to be glorified and God an afterthought.** What I mean by that is, have we ever wondered why so many with so much are so unfulfilled? Have we ever wondered why so many with so little are unfulfilled? Both ends of the spectrum are constantly looking for that "it factor" that seems to not have a name. Sadly enough, I am speaking to churchgoers and non-churchgoers a like.

It is a misnomer to believe that because a person goes to church and worship God that their lives are fulfilled. If that were the case why would so many constantly "dip" out on God to find happiness and then return when their lives are in shambles or they want others to see what they have accomplished. Resolved is that at the end of their day, they are still unhappy and unfulfilled so their cycle of infidelity continues.

The text in Luke reveals a key point that I have often overlooked until now. In order of God to truly build our house, my home, I can't rely on the foundation of the principles I have inherited from my parents. They have passed on an excellent legacy in my humble opinion. However, that is not what God wants us to depend on. Jesus points out in Luke that the foundation must be laid upon the "underlying rock". For me, that was an "aha moment", I never saw that before. Many people build fabulous homes, great families, nice houses, amazing jobs and you name it yet they are unhappy. When you assess their foundation, it was not founded upon an underlying rock. Now days, you can move a house and relocate it down the street or in another state. The question remains, what is it being laid on? I use to tell people who would tell me they wanted to move and start their lives over that moving is great but resolve their problems before going otherwise it's just geography. The same problems they had in one location will go with them to the other location. The travel is not the issue, the relocation is not the issue, and the question to answer is what is all of the decisions based on? What will be the underlying resolve to support the decision or the move?

The more I understand the driving text behind this book, the greater the clarity I have of what God is looking for in me and all of us. ***He wants to be my underlying rock.*** He wants to be the one upon whom my existence lays. It's no wonder so much of what I have experience in the past have met great boulders in the road. I had and still do have great principles, however, not everything has rested on the underlying rock, until now.

As I reflect on the testimonies shared in this book and the journey God has me on, I transparently say do not look for a quick fix to get it right. This book, this inspiration that God has deposited in me is to remind me and to remind you that Psalms 127:1 must be taken seriously in all that we do. It's a journey of discovery. It is a journey of pain for gain. The pain of being taught right yet doing wrong only to then learn from the wrong to gain your footing on the path God initially intended for you to trod. When God is building your home He does not have room for anything beneath your foundation but him.

I reflect back to the work that was being done outside my home. All of what was underneath the soil, the old roots, the pain of the past had to be dug up in order for new ground to be laid. The bit that was shared about my life, the hidden things that I shared with no one until now was hidden because I was ashamed and fearful of speaking. I was so private that I didn't have space to let anyone in, not even God. Did you know that those are the things that creep into your memory banks arresting you from moving forward without realizing it? I remember in some of my low moments, I would fall into a depressive state and question why those things and others happened to me? What did I do to deserve those treatments? My family was great, my life was great, and I received love at all times so why? I had a lot of suppressed feelings growing up and my self-esteem was extremely low. This journey has taught me and continues to teach me that the foundation is only as strong as the underlying rock it rest upon. I get it now.

I love the song by Israel Houghton "Jesus at the center". According to an article I came across on the Internet, "in ancient building practices, the cornerstone was the principal stone placed at the corner of the edifice. The cornerstone was usually one of the largest, the most solid, and the most carefully constructed of any in the edifice. Jesus describes Himself as the Cornerstone that His church would be built upon, a unified body of believers, both Jew and Gentile." In essence, without the cornerstone, the foundation regardless how elaborate it was, would never be able to stand. I love the Lord but as I look back I confess he was a stone that I desperately needed to be the chief cornerstone of my life but because of the unspoken and fear I kept him at bay. I worshipped, I fasted, I prayed and I would say Jesus you are all that I needed. I did not until now; really give him full access to all of me. I was building my house but not on a firm foundation. I must say there is such a shift from when I sang that song before and when I sing it now. When He becomes your chief cornerstone everything is all right. You could be in the middle of a storm and it's all right. You could be at your lowest emotionally and it's alright. Understanding that underlying rock is, for me, knowing the role Jesus MUST play in your life in order for you to stand. Wow! Amen!

The foundation of my ministry was not predicated on the building I was incubated in but the rock I was laid upon. It took me a long time to understand that God placed me in the church where I first pastored not to find a resting place but to find HIM! Let me say it this way. Too many people, especially young ministers, myself included believe that the history of a particular building or church is what is needed to establish you into who God has called you to be. No! God calls us not to a building built by man or a pulpit owned by man. **He calls us to a grace of service that wherever He places us He is the platform and He is the pulpit.** My GOD! Unless the Lord builds your house, it doesn't matter where you are, a building of one or a building of one million as stated in the message bible, you are only building shacks. The ministry will not grow, at least not spiritually under the anointing of the Holy Spirit. The glory of God will not fill the sanctuary. His glory will not shine through your ministry. That underlying rock was the missing piece that God needed to show me but I had to go through in order to grow through.

I mentioned before that my daughter, "my mama" was watching me so I wanted to be more like Jesus in all that I did. I was so desirous of providing the best godly environment for her that I missed the point that the only way to give her what I thought she needed was by getting out of the way and allowing God to heal her brokenness. Erroneously I tried to lay my "parental" foundation upon her solid concrete that covered up a lot of roots that needed to be dug up. When God revealed to me that day that my job was to love her and his would be to correct her, I had such a peace fall over me. I understood that God was building my house. It was not the way I thought it should look. It was not the way I thought it would feel. It was exactly the way He had ordained it. God does not promise us a bed of roses when he is working on us. He does not promise that everything will be perfect in our eyes. We do know though that "all things work together for the good of them who are called according to His purpose." Now that makes sense. The house is built for His purpose not mine, not ours. It doesn't matter if you are a pastor, president or a person on the street. It does matter that we trust God enough to let go. If he says he's got it, He's got it!

The underlying rock for me in my finance was watching how God has positioned my to prosper with little. I worked and earned well before but was never a good steward. My issue was never tithing, that was a given, it was not saying no to those in need. It was looking for ways to make ways for people. I learned that's good but what way have I made for my daughter, my family and myself? I am finding in these areas, that so many work hard, have 401ks, 403bs, life insurance and the list goes on. There is retirement established and the luxurious lifestyle admired and respected by all. The challenge as I have encountered is that on this journey of establishing a solid foundation from which to live so many forget the underlying rock. Some even miss the mark and take claim to fame for what they did, not crediting the one who provides all things. I was reading about King Herod Agrippa in the Book of Acts 12:21-23 NIV.

> [21] and an appointment with Herod was granted. When the day arrived, Herod put on his royal robes, sat on his throne, and made a speech to them. [22] The people gave him a great ovation, shouting, "It's the voice of a god, not of a man!"
>
> [23] Instantly, an angel of the Lord struck Herod with a sickness, because he accepted the people's worship instead of giving the glory to God. So he was consumed with worms and died.

Agrippa made the mistake that so many make today, take the glory for them and forget about the one who put them there in the first place. Never accept the people's worship! Never accept the people's praise. Too many people are tag along and their love is until you fall. They are with you for the season but when the game is over they bid you a gentle goodbye. Worship and praise is your offering to God. Agrippa became consumed with worms because of misdirected praise. When I teach the students in my *"Send Me Program"*, I always tell them that regardless the praise people give you give it back to God. Take no credit for yourself. I am humbled because I see how God has placed upon me a desire to do great exploits for Him but with a character to know that I can't without him. I am at an awesome place in my life where I am doing even more with little than I was able to do with much.

God, as He has me in this place of shift and transformation, is reminding me that how I handle the blessings He pours in me must be founded upon Him. Funny, I always thought I was doing that. I always thought the things I did, the people I blessed leaving myself without was what he wanted. In my reflection I see He was the missing link. Wow! How did that happen? Hard to comprehend even for a servant of God but easy to understand when He puts you on pause to reflect. Jesus! I now see how busy I was doing as opposed to being. I was busy doing right, setting the world right, and making things good for others. I did not pause enough to just be. I did not pause enough to really allow God to envelope me in His arms and let him guide my footsteps in every area of my life. When he called me to ministry it was not because of the finished product but the potential of the promise that was in me. He knew me and ordained me before I was even conceived but he had to take the filth of doing life out of me so that he could be the strength upon which I would rest. He made me and needed me to relax enough so that He could regain the steering wheels of my life. He must guide every bit of me. Wow! I tell you, as you read, it is worth assessing how much of you is lead by you and your ego? Are you so stuck on "your" mission, "your" agenda that you have put God on hold until you have it all figured out? If God does not become the underlying rock in your every situation the storm when it comes will rock your world. In Jamaica they have a saying, "pay me now or pay me later". In other words, give God His now or give it to him later but what is His he will receive. Go willingly or go kicking. When there is a call on your life, you in all your accomplishments can never out do God. You can't out do, out love, out serve, out give, out nothing. God is God!!!! Wow!

The understanding of the foundation of first having peace and then the underlying rock really helped shape purpose. They say you can tell a lot about a person by how they dress. The challenge is I have met too many people with the most expensive attire, flawless make up, and yet they are decaying internally. They are in some ways what Jesus calls "whitewash sepulchers." They say never judge a book by the cover yet it is the cover that is supposed to draw you in, peak your interest in wanting to know more. Irony! **Life continues to teach me the value of not only the cover but also the content.** As is the essence of this book, if God is not the builder of my being then I will only look the part. If God is not the builder of my house there will be no peace and there will be no underlying rock. If God is not the builder of my all, then my service for him will be the banging of instruments that make no meaningful sound. I believe that is what Paul in the book of Corinthians is referring to in terms of baseless worship, a "sounding brass and tinkling cymbal."

Now that the foundation of this stage of my life has been laid upon the underlying rock and there is peace in my purpose I have important decisions to make. You see there comes a point in our walk where God turns it over to us and expects us to make decisions on our own. Now these decisions will no longer be decisions that please us but ones that bring glory to the father. In the book of Psalms 37:4 NIV

> *Take delight in the Lord, and He will give*
> *you the desires of your heart*

In other words, when you put God first in all that you do. When your thoughts are aligned with his, your desires are aligned with his then and only then will you receive what he wants to give you. **Your motives are not laid upon your ego but upon his glory.** You wont want things that will grieve the Holy Spirit. Instead, you will desire things that are good, things that are lovely. Yes your desires actually become like His desires. Too many misunderstand that and try to tell God you said and quote scripture after scripture but when you check, their motive was not about God but themselves. If you dig further, they are not building upon The Rock. God is not the chief cornerstone of their home. He is not the underlying rock of their existence. That's like me going to KFC and wanting a Big Mac. KFC doesn't specialize in Big Macs but I am making a decision that I want to rewrite the purpose of KFC for my good. I want KFC to adjust to me and not the other way around. God will not adjust to me or to you! He is God! If He is not the underlying rock then I can't want from him what he wants to give me. This takes me to the outfitting of the home. When we fall into the will of God then we can rest assured that everything from the columns to the windows, to the paint and furniture we choose will be centered on giving God glory.

Jesus at the Center

I threw the shot put and discuss in high school and college and later became a coach. One of the things I remembered both as an athlete and when I coached was the importance of moving down the center of the ring. You could be the strongest in the field or the quickest but if you were off center coming across the ring you could anticipate a bad throw. It was important as you entered the ring to find the center. The center of the ring helped you to know where to plant your pivot leg. You knew once you hit that point you had to accelerate your speed. You knew once you hit that point that the power of the throw was in flight, a bad plant lead to a bad throw but a good plant had the potential for an amazing throw. A lot was riding on your positioning once you left the back of the ring towards the center. I use this analogy as I think of our relationship with Jesus. A lot is riding on our positioning of him in our lives. He cannot be a thought. He cannot be on the side or left in the back. The power of our purpose rests on him being in the center.

In the construction of a building, the center refers to the main column. Every building has a main column. It is the column from which all the others are positioned. Without it, the building will not hold up. The roof rests on the main column. The walls all come back to the main column. Based on the size on of the building, there might be two or three principal columns. Regardless, there are no walls, decoration furniture, or anything for that matter without them.

Going back to Israel Houghton's song, "Jesus at the Center", I have never met a true worshipper who does not have Jesus at the center. I have met a lot of amazing talent, get you going but without Jesus there is no anointing. **People confuse the emotion of the moment with the presence of God in someone's life.** I believe this is where we miss the mark and this is what the text is telling us. If God is not the builder even of the ministry that He gave to you then your emotion will bless and glorify your flesh but your spirit man will be found wanting. The emotion of the moment causes even the sinner to feel good and forget they are living in sin. The word of God says, "They that worship me must worship me in spirit and in truth." You can't worship in spirit and definitely not in truth if you are living a lie. Sounds harsh but let's be real. If God is building your home how can you party all night and then get up on the pulpit to say raise your hands everyone, the devil is a lie.

In the Book of Judges 16:25-30 NIV, Samson in a weakened state teaches us the power of the central column.

> [25] While they were in high spirits, they shouted, "Bring out Samson to entertain us." So they called Samson out of the prison, and he performed for them.
>
> When they stood him among the pillars, [26] Samson said to the servant who held his hand, "Put me where I can feel the pillars that support the temple, so that I may lean against them." [27] Now the temple was crowded with men and women; all the rulers of the Philistines were there, and on the roof were about three thousand men and women watching Samson perform. [28] Then Samson prayed to the LORD, "Sovereign LORD, remember me. Please, God, strengthen me just once more, and let me with one blow get revenge on the Philistines for my two eyes." [29] Then Samson reached toward the two central pillars on which the temple stood. Bracing himself against them, his right hand on the one and his left hand on the other, [30] Samson said, "Let me die with the Philistines!" Then he pushed with all his might, and down came the temple on the rulers and all the people in it. Thus he killed many more when he died than while he lived.

It was so critical that he be placed between those columns, no other column would do. The destruction of the Philistines was predicated on him being placed between those two columns. In similar fashion, the defeat of the enemy of our souls is predicated on Jesus being the center of our lives. We do not have the personal strength to fight the enemy on our own. But God! It is His strength that is greater and we only experience it when He is center. We only experience it when He is our builder and not we ourselves.

It would be so easy at this point to speak in theory and highlight all of what one must do moving forward in order to complete the construction of the house. It would be so easy to research what builders do and put together a formula for you to follow, a model to live by. Sadly enough we live in a prepackaged age where EVERYTHING is prepackaged. Not many take the time to invest time, patience and the necessary energy to see your plan succeed. After such an awesome, mind blowing season of shift in my life, I am moving at a cautious intentional pace. Isaiah 40:28-31 NIV

> [28] *Do you not know? Have you not heard? The* LORD *is the everlasting God, the Creator of the ends of the earth. He will not grow tired or weary, and his understanding no one can fathom.* [29] *He gives strength to the weary and increases the power of the weak.* [30] *Even youths grow tired and weary, and young men stumble and fall;* [31] *but those who hope in the* LORD *will renew their strength. They will soar on wings like eagles; they will run and not grow weary, they will walk and not be faint.*

That waiting is at a pace of surrender. I have been guilty and have heard others say that they waited on the Lord and haven't heard from him. I wonder about that at times because the God that we serve is faithful and His word says he wont deny us any good thing. So If we are waiting on God and he has not so much as batted an eye, is it what we asked for or that he answered but it is not what we wanted? I dare not give an answer but we do need to evaluate this thought. If we really want God to build, did he already give an answer but we were not satisfied. Do we know that NO is an answer as well. Are we okay that access denied could be

God's positioning us for His yes or access granted? I think that is a cause for pause moment.

What God is revealing to me in this process and I share with you is that everything down to the color of the cushion is inspired by a thought that comes from Him, when He is the true center. Even when you believe you are the one picking it out, pause to consider who inspired you to go to that store on that day to get that discount which in turn saved you money.

In the areas of ministry, family, relationships, finances and more, God has taken center stage. Those things or people that he moved out of my life are not fixtures in this new construction. My columns are different as are the walls, windows and furnishing. My approach to situations has taken on a form that looks nothing like me some years ago. When I stand to declare the word of God I am not sure who that person is. I am resting on the Underlying Rock and it feels amazing.

I share this for someone reading as God would not let me let it go as I write. Lazarus lay in the tomb for four days. When Jesus raised him from the dead and called him out a few things had to happen. The men on the outside, those who placed the stone over the tomb, consider them part of the obstacle or hindrance to you reaching your goal had to go and remove them at Jesus' command. Did you know God would use the very ones who blocked you to bless you? When Lazarus came out, Jesus told them to remove the wrappings. Why is this important? Those wrappings were a hindrance to his forward moving. They were dead clothes, dead weight, and things of the past. They were the things that were buried under the concrete and now that it is opened and they are exposed they need to be uprooted. When your house is founded upon the Rock, your decisions on columns and fixtures will move you away from the grave clothes.

My distant spiritual father, Bishop TD Jakes gave a teaching once on leadership and it has weighed heavily on how I now operate in ministry and in life. He spoke about three groups of people:

Confidants, Constituents and Comrades. The confidants are in that small circle we all have. They are with you regardless your situation and you can count on them. They will tell you are wrong and love you the same. They are honest and not interested in impressing or being impressed. Secondly, the constituents are the ones who are with you because you are going in the same direction but not necessarily with you. Should the storm hit, like it did with me, they may jump ship to another that will get them to where they are going. For them it is nothing personal, they were never with "you". Finally, the comrades are with you because you share a common enemy. The thing about the comrades is once the enemy is gone; they will turn on you quickly. When I saw this again following my storm, I gained great peace. When you put things and people in their rightful place, you never come up wounded, bothered yes, but not wounded.

The challenge moving forward is as your new house is being built, how do you decide which group is which in your personal life, in your home, in your ministry and on the job? How do you make key decisions on the partitions of your home and where things will go moving forward? The answer is simple. Let God build. Let God lead. Let God be in his rightful place, center of it all.

My core fixture is a thirst for more of God. Jesus says in John 17:22 NIV

> "22 I have given them the glory that you gave me, that they may be one as we are one"

I am so hungry for more of His glory. I am thirsty with an insatiable thirst for more of Him. I have watched how, though slowly, everything is falling into place not as I would have thought it but how God has designed it. The onlooker lacking faith might not see the hand of God, but when I look back and see where God has brought me from and I look ahead and know he has a plan for my life I just say thank you. You should try that. **Stop allowing your past to consume your present.** God has new columns stored up for each of you but he needs to become that underlying rock so that he can truly bless you.

In 2014 I was in the Dominican Republic at a Prayer Conference that I host there and I stayed at the home of one of the Pastors, tremendous woman of God. One night after service, the Lord was not done and we were just praising Him. He spoke a word to her that confirmed a message I preached in Guatemala a few years back, "Do not despise the small beginnings." For those who are unfamiliar with this scripture, it comes from the Book of Zechariah 4:10 NIV

> *[10] "Who dares despise the day of small things, since the seven eyes of the LORD that range throughout the earth will rejoice when they see the chosen capstone in the hand of Zerubbabel?"*

The older children of Israel who were familiar with the great temple built by King Solomon were disheartened following the Babylonian captivity when God instructed them to rebuild the temple in Jerusalem. Their vision was set on what was and not what God was going to do. At one point they even abandoned the work to focus on their own lives and God sent them a word. Did you know that when God gives you a directive and you take a detour he will send a word? In the King James translation, the text does not ask a question but gives a command, "Don't despise the days of small beginnings…" It does not matter how it looks to us, when it connects with the glory of God great things can happen. Elija's servant saw the cloud the size of a man's hand and Elija dared to declare abundance of rain.

What she shared was that God was going to use small beginnings to do a great work through me. My breaking as she shared was that it not only rested on where I was in my spirit but also strengthened me to stand even taller in the center of my storm. Sometimes, because of our nature and wanting things grandiose at the onset, we lose the blessing of the small beginnings.

I remember once listening to Dr. Juanita Bynum give her testimony of the trials she has experienced in life and how

God pulled her through. In her moments of alone and feeling of abandonment, God was with her. This really impacted me because the lengthy season that I just came out of was God preparing me to step into this next level of glory, but it was painful. I embraced the reality that not everyone or thing in your life gets the invitation to join at the next level. It then becomes a stripping away that is involuntary because in my case, you want God's will. Yet, it is involuntary because His will means He decides who stays and who goes. As I mentioned elsewhere, God has removed people and relationships form my life. The spotlight when on and suddenly as in a dark room when the light goes on, everything/one scatters. I am talking about those who would hug you, kiss you, tell you they love you just scatter. There was a shift in my time in terms of where and how I spent it. It was painful but necessary. Now I stand on a foundation of such great peace. I am at a place you do not make up nor dream up, you have to grow through.

ARTIFACT #5

Waiting

It is so easy to open the catalogue of someone's life and shop for answers to your situation. It is easy to want to sit under someone to get a temporary fix to your long-term problem. It is so easy to look at another person's outcome and covet it for yourself. That is a sin by the way! A covetous spirit will never get you closer to God. In the words of Dr. Juanita Bynum, "I don't mind waiting"

"You, know, sometimes in life, situations are going to occur where you may look to the left or the right and you can't find any answers and you can't find anybody to help you but I'm reminded of the Word that says they that wait upon the Lord, He shall renew their strength. They shall mount up on wings as eagles. They shall run and not be weary. They shall walk and not faint. Come on. You've got to learn how to wait."

I don't mind waiting.

I don't mind waiting.

I don't mind waiting, on You Lord.

I don't mind waiting.

I don't mind waiting.

I don't mind waiting, on You Lord.

When God begins to realize His purpose in our lives and we have established that He is the foundation, the underlying rock of our existence, let us not rush him. Let us take from Dr. Bynum and grow a little patience.

I remember in my earlier years, I would be in a hurry to get something done. My mom would have me clean and I would "pala pala". In Jamaica that means to clean the visible in a careless way that it "looks" good but if you go up close. Have you ever just wanted to be done with something so you can move on to the next thing? The tragedy with that approach to things is that it can spill over into your personal and spiritual life as well.

I was in a hurry to "fix" my nutcracker. I was in a hurry to get "Pastoring" right. Is that possible? I was in a hurry to get life right. I was moving fast without realizing the speed. This is so important because the building and shaping of this next level of blessing will require of me, as it will you that you establish a garden of patience. There is virtue in patience; there is virtue in waiting. There is virtue in being still in the Lord. When you try to do things outside of the will God you end up paying a higher price than you would by simply waiting. This sounds easy I know but I am not speaking from a text or another person's story. This is my journey in the Lord being used to encourage you who are still asking the question "what did I do wrong?" You are still wondering why you have not gotten further in life, passed up for the promotion or overlooked for the last contract.

The key to the Isaiah's text of waiting on the Lord is that you are not waiting on man. Man will not and cannot determine the outcome of this construction when God is at the center. When He is the chief cornerstone. I don't care who you are or the title you carry, God both precedes and follows after. He is the beginning and the end. There was none before him or will there be any after him. If He is the almighty, can anything or anyone trump His decision? So capturing that thought, it allows walking in peace and the confidence that if God said it, He will do it. That is what has slowed me down. That is what will slow you down, if you let Him. That understanding that you too can reach the height He wants to take you if you let him. So after you have gone through some stuff like I mentioned earlier in this book. After you have gone through some stuff like Dr. Bynum mentioned you could look anyone or any opposition in the eye and tell them *"I don't mind waiting on the Lord."*

Consider this, "Except the Lord builds the house, they labor in vain that build it." Can God build your house if you are going faster than Him? I gave an analogy once in a bible study. I said consider yourself on the expressway and God is driving 45 mph. If you try to go 50 mph you are moving outside of the will of God. You need to watch the speed limit of faith and know where God is in your life for that season. It is okay to understand that He is taking you somewhere but do not try to get ahead of Him. I don't mind waiting on the Lord!

DEDICATION AND POSSESSION PHASE III

Lord Bless This House

One of the things I enjoy doing as a pastor is being invited to bless someone's home after they have purchased it. I love to see the body of Christ blessed but more so when they understand the importance of blessing their home. Symbolically they are telling the Lord that they want give back to him what he has given to them. In the Book of Deuteronomy 6:4-9, we see the home as a sacred place. Israel was instructed to teach their children from home the laws of God. The home was where the priest, the head of the home resided and he was to lead his family into worship. That being said, a home where the Word of God was a blessed home as is today.

Another reason why I have been invited to some homes has been to temper the spiritual atmosphere. Homes that have been occupied by different groups of individuals with different spiritual practices will with time experience spiritual battles. The truth is, it does not have to go that far. Who are you letting in your home? What practices have you given permission to in your home? **When God is the builder of your home there has to be the smell of holiness there.** It must look different, feel different and spiritually be different. The blessing of the home is saying, " I want the Holy Spirit to be welcome here." I want this place to be the place where God dwells.

When King Solomon was building the temple for God, the glory of God came down and filled it as they worshipped. God told King Solomon that he would reside in that place. Because it was a blessed house, God told him when they sinned or fell short they could return to that place and be restored. A blessed house is a place of restoration and hope. When your house is blessed, God's glory will fill the place. People will walk in and comment that there is such peace in your home. I love being in your home, you can feel the presence of God here. You might ask, "If God is the center, the underlying rock, why do you need to then bless? " Well, if God created you why do you have to invite him into your heart? He is the Sovereign Lord but he will not force himself on anyone even if who you are and where you are is because of His goodness. The decision you make is will you take credit for you and your possession or will you return it to him? When you keep it, you are glorified and that's your reward. But when you give it to Jesus it doesn't matter the challenges you might face even after the blessing, you will have the peace of knowing God's got it. So you bless your home so God can have it. Besides, isn't it awesome just to know that if it belongs to God there will be no want, you will not lack anything because the owner is the provider? My God!

When God gave me my home everything about it was a miracle. If you know my full story you would know there is no way I should have it, more in my next book. I told the Lord, and this is what many don't understand, that if He gave it to me I would give it back to him. I was renting first, that was also a miracle, and when it was time to make a decision I put it to prayer. I knew I was unworthy but if he wanted me to have it He would have to lead me on how. He would have to open the doors because alone I would not be able to. God placed in my path not only the people but He was so strategic that even the closing was ridiculous, divinely ridiculous, that's another story. Before I signed the paperwork for possession of the land, I had a prayer vigil and returned the house to God. Yes, I was not the owner yet but I had a prayer of surrender to God before the closing telling the Lord this was his house. My home is now headquarters for the church I pastor. It was the place where Flowing Rivers International Church was birthed.

It has become the place where a myriad of activities for

the church take place. It is the place where I provide council and mentor the body. It belongs to God.

As you reflect back to the earlier chapters where I share the challenges and wanting God to be the underlying rock, the storms that have passed the pain of the journey one might say how is that possible? Well because the house is blessed in the midst of it all, the God has been the center. God has been the healer, the provider the peace in the midst of trial. It has become the place of great crying out to an almighty God and each time He has been there to respond. He did not promise that there would not be challenges, He promised to not leave me or abandon me during those challenges. He could do so freely because I gave him full access. The underlying rock of my natural and spiritual house is the Lord and because of that He has become my builder. This was not clear to me until this journey began and with the clarity has come strength and boldness.

I encourage every reader who lives in a space regardless the size. Take a moment and ask yourself the question. Did I bless this home? Is God the center? I am not talking about the problems you are facing or the stressful life you lead. Is God the center, have you blessed it yet? If not, call you prayer leader or your pastor and invite them to come over. Let them know you want to give your home to the Lord. Understand that means some cleaning will take place before during and after the process. This call is to say because I want a life in Christ and I want Jesus to be the underlying rock of this home, I am ready to through out and shut down those things that are displeasing to him. It might hurt but it's important. Why am I saying all of this? The Word says you cannot put new wine into old wine skin or you cannot pour new joy on top of old pain. The new joy wont last because the old pain will pierce through. As soon as you want to celebrate the new a memory or flashback that you have not released comes back and consumes you. So it IS time to clean house. Go ahead. Make the call. I know you want the blessing. Ok try this analogy, think about where God has brought you. Now put all that pain, all that hurt, all that sorrow in your arms and pick up a baby. You have placed a newborn baby who has done no wrong in arms filled with baggage they do not deserve. Now you want to show them love but you cant because of the weight in your arms. The baby may not only sense it but also become resistant. But if you release the weight before picking them up, there is a lightness and joy that comes over you both. A home filled with the pain of the past cannot have the same joy and peace as one that has been rid of it because it was released in the hands of God.

This analogy is not just for the physical home. Your body is to become the temple of almighty God. If you have confessed Jesus Christ as your Lord and Savior, you are doing the same thing as your physical home. You are saying to God, I want to make you Lord of my life. I want you to be the builder of my life. I want you to be the underlying rock of my existence. He cannot and will not intrude unless you let him in. He says he is standing at the door and he is knocking. It is your decision if you are going to open the door and let him in. Once you make that decision you are telling him, "I have thought about it and I am ready to release the baggage of my past. I know I was not living right. I was living in sin. I am a sinner due to the fall of man but now I want to be free. I want you to take over. I want you to be Lord of my life." Those are powerful words but if you are serious, He will do it. It does not mean you wont go through challenges but like the house, He's got this!

If you really want God to build your home you have to give it back to him. Go back to the tools. Have you ever seen the ground that is being worked on holding the tool that is working on it? No! So if God is to become the builder of your home, release the tools and invite the builder to come in.

Everywhere You Go

For some people the dedication takes place after the possession of the home or the property but in this case it does not. It does not for me because, as many of those who know me, I have crazy faith. I actually believe God's word. **I actually believe if God says it He will do it.** You should too! The Word says in Mark 11:22-24 NIV

> [22] *"Have faith in God," Jesus answered.* [23] *"Truly I tell you, if anyone says to this mountain, 'Go, throw yourself into the sea,' and does not doubt in their heart but believes that what they say will happen, it will be done for them.* [24] *Therefore I tell you, whatever you ask for in prayer, believe that you have received it, and it will be yours.*

So our prayer cannot be filled with doubt or our desires for the things of God. I believe it is good to begin giving thanks to God for the things we cannot see before we see it. Isn't that faith? When you take God at his word even when you cannot see it or feel it. **He says he will heal you from that migraine so stop babying it and taking ownership of it as though you cannot live without it.** If you want to be healed and God said he would heal you start thanking him. I am not crazy just experienced. I was in Guatemala one year and fell down a few stairs badly twisting my ankle. It was the type of twist where it became freezing cold first and then the pain gushed out consuming the entire ankle, foot, and body or so it felt. Those who came to my rescue wanted to rush me off to the hospital. It was bad! At my request they helped me to my room as they prepared ice. I refused to go to the hospital thinking I am in a foreign country, I leave in a few days and then it hit me. I had oil and I had the Word. God told me if I asked ANYTHING in His name he would do it. He told me he would heal me. He told me I just needed faith. I grabbed the oil, laid my hand on that ankle and went to work. No, it was not an instant thing where the pain went away. But in my spirit man I knew God had healed me. I took God at his word. To make a long story short, the physical pain lasted several weeks but my faith grew. Each time I felt it I reminded God and thanked him for his goodness. To this day I have not gone to the doctor for my ankle. That was my faith, yours might be different but His word is the same regardless.

Now in the book of Joshua, I chose that because we can talk about so many other cases in the bible where God made limitless promises. Everywhere your foot goes, as far as your eyes can see, or any you ask in Jesus's name. He made promises that were and still are beyond the scope of the limited capacity of our reasoning. In Joshua, God told him that he had already given him the land and all he had to do; all Israel had to do was to go and posses it.

> *I promise you what I promised Moses: Everywhere you go, you will be on land I have given you. Joshua 1:3 NIV*

If we can grasp just his verse alone, we will gladly let go and let God build our land. Israel had not yet crossed the Jordan. Joshua had not yet circumcised them. They had not yet marched around the wall of Jericho a visually impossible victory. Yet, God told them that he had already given them the land. He told them everywhere their foot touches would be theirs. **All they had to do was believe.** All they had to do was walk. All they had to do was trust God. What has God promised you but because you looked with the natural eyes and not the spiritual eyes you did not see what God had for you? God says in his word that his promises are yes and amen meaning they are final. All Israel had to do was obey the laws of Moses, the Word of God and walk in faith by stepping of the promises of God. What comes to mind is that many people are afraid of blessing before seeing.

In Jamaica we would say "don't jinx it" don't curse it by speaking before it's time. Was there a storm before Elijah's servant saw the cloud the size of a man's hand? No! Did Israel have the land before crossing the Jordan? No! Did Abraham have a nation before his barren wife Sarah had her son at age 90? No! But if God said it He will fulfill it. The only thing that must be certain is that He is the builder, the underlying rock upon which all that you are rests. He promised it, you just have to obey and give thanks.

This is the part where people get a little confused in the possession because God said it is theirs they just sit and wait for it to happen. God said he would bless me so I am going to take it easy. Israel had to fight; they had to get rid of the enemy that occupied their land. You see, when God promised it to them, that was now their home. They now had a duty to clean their home, ridding it of anything that would cause them to have unrest. They were going home to live in peace, to rest from a long journey. You can't live with the enemy. Light and dark cannot inhabit the same space. One has to go.

Possession is an ongoing process. You take action to own and you take action to maintain. Have you ever lived in a place where you do nothing? Day one it is clean and smelling good. You feel great until day 365 after you have done no work, no maintenance. The furniture is falling apart; there is an odor that rises up. You have become so use to it that you don't even notice it. Filth has infiltrated and now it possesses your home instead of you as you did on day one. The same is true with your body, which is the temple of God. When you ask God to take over, if you do not feed it by keeping it sin free in a very short time you are back to the old life without realizing that you have evicted the Lord.

When you dedicate your home, your temple, you are no longer the owner. God becomes the owner and the Holy Spirit challenges you to maintain it. I say challenge but I refer to a spirit of conviction. That which is Holy can never be at peace in midst of something or someone who is unholy. It doesn't work. When God builds He orders your steps.

The Lord makes firm the steps of the one who delights in him; Psalms 37:23 NIV

When you delight in God meaning that He is the builder, He guides you in all your ways. He shows you which doors to go through and which to stay away from. He reveals to you what furniture, people, will pour into you and which will suck you dry. He gives you strength to cut the chord of the thing that is killing your blessing and the faith to move forward.

I ask you this, is it possible we are afraid to bless it first because we were raised not to "jinx" it? We were raised to not count the chickens before they are hatched. You have to work for what you want, and you do. But there is a difference when your efforts are because of the flesh as opposed to the spirit. Your work is not in vain when God is leading. Don't get me wrong, because God revealed to you your blessing does not give you permission to get ahead of him, set up shop and start building without first making him the builder. He gave you a glimpse so you can rest on the promise of what is to come while in the meantime positioning yourself to be blessed. **It's the readiness factor.**

The readiness factor for me is like the 10 virgins in Luke 12:35-39. All of them were waiting for the Bridegroom to return, representative of Jesus. Five of them went prepared in anticipation that they might have to wait a long time so they had extra oil. Five of them, however, just had enough. When he finally came, the five foolish were nowhere to be found because they left to look for more oil. They were not ready. The five wise on the other hand were ready and went in with the bridegroom. That is such huge lesson on faith and salvation. We can't say God said it but I am going to wait until I see it. If He said it he will fulfill it. It's a matter of believing. It is a matter of faith. It is a matter of being lead by Him. Not seeing a thing doesn't mean it doesn't exist. Not knowing when it will happen does not mean it will not happen. God told Adam that the seed of the woman would crush the head of the serpent. Jesus came to fulfill that promise.

Agree with me: Father, right now, for every person that is reading this section I pray. I pray that their faith is strengthened. I believe Lord that you purposed in their heart to read this book because you are about to outpour your glory upon them. I declare in the name of Jesus that the lies that they were fed are now broken, the chains of pain have been broken; the yoke of history has been cast off. I release over them new insight into your purpose for their lives. Lord I ask that as they enter this new season with great hesitation that you will give them the strength to move forward. I pray a release of blessings over their home, their family, their finance and their journey in you. I pray increased faith in the name of Jesus. Lord, it is by the power of your Holy Ghost that I declare all this done in Jesus' Name. Amen!

Faith to Rise

If you just said that prayer with me, let us move forward, rising up into a new day, a new you. When you have been through a storm that leaves you feeling lifeless, you do not have much to hold on to. It should be that nothing could motivate you to stand up. Funny, I always preached and taught that I left the field of education after 17 ½ years not because I wanted to become a Pastor; I did not. I repeat I did NOT! I left because God told me my time was up. He had waited long enough and he brought me to Massachusetts not to function in the capacity I did but to position me for His purpose. **Let me tell you, when you are positioned for God's purpose you have an attitude like the writer says "none of these things move me".** Man will never be able to understand it unless you have walked this walk I am describing.

I was on the Damascus road of life, not in rebellion to God but not focusing on anything that remotely looked like what I am doing now. This does not diminish the pain of the process by any means. The point is that where others might have jumped ship, held up a fight or gone in a different direction, God allowed me to stand firm. The pieces of the puzzle were falling into place and I was not the puzzle maker. My God!

The decision was reached that my first assignment as pastor was no longer a perfect fit and respectfully I agree. As mentioned before, a baby cannot stay connected to the umbilical chord once it's left the womb. Both the baby and the mother would be affected. I had reached new level in my call and it was my time to morph into the full purpose of my mission here in New England. The pain of goodbye is real but the joy of the next level made it less traumatic.

I received a bold confirmation on September 22, 2014 that my call truly was from God. I went home and the individuals who have prayed me through many moments came to my home not to show pity but to show strength. We went into a time of prayer. Right away God made it clear, new beginning. A couple days later we met and we prayed. We have not stopped praying. God led us to the book of Ezekiel and from there we received the name of the church "Flowing Rivers International Church." Everywhere the river flowed it brought life. God had given us new life and we would become the conduits through which other lives would be revived.

I felt like in addition to that, God was also challenging me. Along with that bold confirmation I mentioned earlier it was as though God was saying now I need you to prove me. You have preached it, you have taught it, now live it. It was like Jesus speaking to Peter where he asked him three times if he loved him and with each response of yes, Jesus told him to feed his sheep. Well, this is only my second honor of serving as Pastor for a congregation but this time around I see where so many of the preaching God allowed me to deliver spoke about a shift and little did I know it would lead to first being birthed and then birthing something from within.

That season was awesome! The word "awesome" for some may come across to be filled with excitement and joy. For me, there was some of that but I am also considering the fact that by definition it also refers to something that is daunting or overwhelming. The season was awesome because it was bigger than me. I appreciated God reminding me of just how awesome He is and reliant I am on him.

It becomes a testimony to me to get over myself. If God is in control then He's got it. Nothing happens without His permission. This was a good painful time because the builder had regained the tools and was working this out for His glory. Faith to rise is the idea of knowing God has regained the tools. Get up out of your situation and stop the pity party. God IS God and if you trust him I mean really trust him let him finish what He started. I believe a lot of people when they go through moments like these look for a reason to blame. They give access to the enemy of our souls. He goes in and brings of things that God has already delivered you from and before long you are in a cave, buried under a rock. My challenge to you is to acknowledge the builder and trust His decision if bricks need to be removed, windows need to be sealed or doors need to be shut. Trust him to repave the driveways of your home giving way to new connections, new opportunities and bigger blessing. Is it possible that the place you were in did not have room for the magnitude of the blessing that was coming your way? Is it possible that your blessing could have been aborted had you stayed and fought trying to put a square peg in a round hole? Pick your head up, walk with grace and dignity and let God have the final say.

ARTIFACT #6

"Still I Rise"
by Maya Angelou

I absolutely love Dr. Maya Angelou's work. I used to memorize her poems and recite them in school and when appropriate during church activities. One of my favorites is *Still I Rise*. It's the kind of real talk that speaks to your regardless. Regardless the circumstance, I rise. Regardless the pain, I rise. Regardless: you fill in the blank, I rise. Nothing in life will have permission to hold me down; I rise.

Still I Rise

by Maya Angelou
You may write me down in history
With your bitter, twisted lies,
You may tread me in the very dirt
But still, like dust, I'll rise.

Does my sassiness upset you?
Why are you beset with gloom?
'Cause I walk like I've got oil wells
Pumping in my living room.

Just like moons and like suns,
With the certainty of tides,
Just like hopes springing high,
Still I'll rise.

Did you want to see me broken?
Bowed head and lowered eyes?
Shoulders falling down like teardrops.
Weakened by my soulful cries.

Does my haughtiness offend you?
Don't you take it awful hard
'Cause I laugh like I've got gold mines
Diggin' in my own back yard.

You may shoot me with your words,
You may cut me with your eyes,
You may kill me with your hatefulness,
But still, like air, I'll rise.

Does my sexiness upset you?
Does it come as a surprise
That I dance like I've got diamonds
At the meeting of my thighs?

Out of the huts of history's shame
I rise
Up from a past that's rooted in pain
I rise
I'm a black ocean, leaping and wide,
Welling and swelling I bear in the tide.
Leaving behind nights of terror and fear
I rise
Into a daybreak that's wondrously clear
I rise
Bringing the gifts that my ancestors gave,
I am the dream and the hope of the slave.
I rise
I rise
I rise.

This poem is so encouraging when you consider the message of understanding your true worth. **You cannot be a true child of God, know who He is and undervalue your worth acting as a pauper.** You may not look like the next person but if you look like Jesus you understand that you can in fact raise your head high in the midst of your circumstance convicted that God's got it. When God speaks into our lives, when he promises us the land don't expect him to bring it to us. He told Joshua wherever their foot touch would be theirs. There were no boundaries, all they had to do was keep walking. Sometimes we get weary in the journey and satisfied with the little we have. God didn't tell us to stop, we did. If we are to possess the land men and women of God, don't stop at the doors of your sanctuary or your intellectual capacity. Go back out and through your net on the other side and let God fill your troughs. Rise up out of your own self-imposed, self accepted ashes and step into your blessing. Your builder is not finite so reach beyond the scope of your finite thinking into the possibility of the impossibility. It is there that your faith is tested; it is there that you see God.

138

LESSONS LEARNED FINAL PHASE IV

You know you are changed when not much moves you. You know you are not the same when the things that would bother you no longer do. You know you have shifted when the people who you used to call on or who called on you no longer moved you. You just get to a place of, well God it's you and me. I now cry less from pain and more from blessing. I cry, you sing, because I'm happy. Wait! What am I talking about? From the outside things don't look so good. From the outside my home is not perfect. From the outside there is a lot of work to be done. Yes!!! That's just it. If God is the builder it doesn't mean that from the outside things looks perfect, it means He is perfecting you from the inside out. Wow! That hit me! I spend hours listening to people and mentoring them in their situation. I speak to them with authority of the Word! Today, I speak from a place of confident vulnerability. Confident because if God did it for me I know he can do it for them. Vulnerability because I know I am under constant construction but the foundation has been established.

In this entire journey, God has taught me to stand in my pain, to smile in the face of opposition, and to praise through when I can't pray though and vice versa. He has allowed me to be an even greater example to my household, my nutcracker and my nephew who has since made the shift to a newlywed. I celebrate more now in the truth that where God is there is peace, there is joy, there is love and the list goes on. Where I was at the beginning of the journey I am where God wants me to be right now. I am resting! Ah, it feels good.

It was good that I had been afflicted.

It was good that I had been afflicted is a form of appreciation and understanding that affliction is not always a bad thing especially when God is the builder. This is not an original thought but rather what the Psalmist stated in Psalm 119:71:

It was good for me to be afflicted so that I might learn your decrees.

It is an understanding that the lesson was not learned until after the affliction. When our parents tell us not to touch the hot stove and we do it just to rebel or see what the big deal was, we learn quickly that the hot stove will burn us. The next time we move away from it while it is hot and proceed with caution so as not to experience the same pain as before.

It was over a year ago that the Lord brought me to the underlying text of this book and something so simple was difficult for me to wrap my head around. It was not to be a well-scripted sermon but one that would arrest my fears and give birth to a new day in my life. From this one verse, unless God builds my house the work is in vain has taken on new meaning for me and prayerfully for you as well. I began talking about the perfect storm which lead to a great deal of uprooting, exposing, building and shaping leading to a point of blessing and possessing. This lesson could not have been taught in the classroom. It should not be preached baselessly, used only as filler from the pulpit to tell people how to live their lives. I dare to declare if every preacher, teacher, minister or leader had this foundation as the basis for which their ministry or home is built we would not use the bible as a hammer but as an umbrella. We would not arrest people on the dos and don'ts but cover them under the love of God and allow the warmth of His love change their lives and hearts. I saw once where someone stated that they have met more nice people with tattoos and piercings than people in the church. That is sad! This is not a judgment call on appearance but a sad truth that God must be the builder of our homes. Regardless of how we want to justify the definition of home we can understand that if it is the place of dwelling, the place of worship or our hearts, He must be the builder. God is love; therefore we stand to heal more than hurt when He is the underlying rock.

This season has taught me more about this call that has been placed upon my life, the responsibilities that accompany it. Funny, I have four degrees and a couple certificates and still I was unprepared to fill this shoe as Senior Pastor yet God called me. I will not use this or any medium to judge right or wrong academic preparation to serve in this capacity. What I will say is regardless the level of preparation of anyone if God is not the builder of your home He is not God over your life. From the most accomplished to the unaccomplished, this lesson has taught me through great affliction that He builds, He leads, and I follow.

This affliction has given me greater patience and understanding of how to parent my now 20-year-old "nutcracker". I do not want her to look like anyone because she is with the Pastor. I do not want her to believe she has to be a certain way because she is with the Pastor. I do not want her to miss the opportunity of freewill because she is with the Pastor. I just want her to understand that there is a God who loves her and will never leave her nor forsake her. I give the church community permission to love her in correction and love her out of correction, not to make her look traditional but to help her as she walks along God's highway of life. ***I was so stuck on what others might say that I almost missed out on simply being her "Nina".*** God is now building our home in this area.

I find I am now able to really speak with parents who approach me on their children or loved ones. My approach is not from a high seat but from a face to face, eye to eye, I understand where you are. If God did it for me, he can do it for you. Let's agree in prayer for your situation. A word to the reader, it is challenging to agree in prayer on something you do not believe in.

In ministry, I am in heaven. God has given me a family of believers that keeps me on my toes because they are so hungry. I feel like mom, sister, aunt, grandma, teacher, preacher and everything in between. While we are a young ministry God positioned us from day one with practically every area of ministry covered. I learned the love of God the first day of service, September 25th, when 52 people who I did not call but who heard we were meeting showed up. We have been growing ever since. Through my affliction I embraced my call. When God is the one who calls you and is your builder He stands true to what Jesus said to Peter, "upon this rock I will build my church and the gates of hell shall not prevail." ***Your call is not incumbent upon a building but rather surrender to his leading.*** As believers and especially servants of God we really must have a Job mentality, you came naked into this world and be prepared to leave naked if you must but never give up on the one who created you. Hold fast, unwavering in your faith.

It was good that I had been afflicted in my finances. That was painful. However, the truth is, while I am qualified to work great jobs my heart is totally surrendered to God. I could have walked away and returned to the system. I did not. I told the Lord He called me, He knew my heart, He was my Jehovah Jirreh and He needed to provide for me. He taught me, he would do all of that but first he would help me to be rich with little to then be able to embrace the blessing that was on its way. Now that was a challenge. I have always been blessed and those who know me have been partakers in my blessing. This journey was part of the process of really letting go of what I could do and leaning on who I knew. I called on Jesus. Praise God! He gave me such peace that the average person would have lost their mind. I just held on and said amen. I was finally able to really let go of the thought of "I have an out with my credentials" and told my parents and some others that all I wanted to do was live for the Lord. That's it! What he wants me to do; where he wants to take me I am there.

This affliction has revealed to me the burden of truth in terms of the love of the Lord and the love of man. While a topic for another book, I am so thankful for this journey because when your house is being built, you can decide who influences the decisions you make for your good. If God is the underlying rock, you can now allow him to really say yes appoint, yes anoint, and the list goes on. A house that is already built has little room for change. But a new construction is built in accordance to the specks of the builder and chief architect. Sometimes we hold on to old construction when God wants to bless us with something new. Sometimes we latch on to old wineskin preventing us from really getting the new anointing. I am thankful for this season of affliction in ministry because my hunger for more has shifted to a level I cannot explain. This book would not have been birthed had I not gone through this affliction. Flowing Rivers International Church, which was never even a concept before would not have been birthed had it not been for this affliction. Terika Smith Ministries with all the conferences now aligned would not have been birthed had it not been for this affliction. The direction of the Send Me Ministries Program for Ministers would not have progressed as it has had it not been for this affliction. I thank God! He gets the glory! It was truly good that I had been afflicted because now I understand more of who I am in Christ and who He is in me.

In my family, I am more open in conversations with where I am. I am still a recluse but I have found a voice and am not afraid to speak. It's a voice of encouragement and challenge. Have you ever been desperate to want your loved ones to experience the blessing you are experiencing? I saw how God was now opening doors for dialogue on another level. Everyone of my family members had the opportunity to weigh in on the cover of my book, that's awesome. While we live in different states, I see healing in the air. God is awesome!

I speak to every reader who cowards down to affliction and believe it should not happen to you. Wrong!! It should happen to you because out of it God has a great work for you to do. Lives are depending on you to heal from your affliction. Souls are to be won as a result of your affliction. I know it hurt going through. I know it is difficult to even discuss where you are. But as I tell my students, get out to the way and let God be God over your life. Be transparent with him but don't move on without Him.

God blocked it

In the church I grew up in after migrating to this country, we used to sing this song:

> *Don't give up on the brink of a miracle*
> *Don't give up, God is still on the throne*
> *Don't give upon the brink of a miracle*
> *Don't give up, remember you are not alone*

Encouraging words like these are meaningless if you do not believe God is still on the throne. It is easy to say is there a God, or does he even care about me? It is easy to ask why he allowed this to happen to me? It is also okay in your pain to ask the questions and to get frustrated. However, it is not okay to stay in that place.

In one of my earlier rants, I shared some of the dark moments in my life. These were moments that I was not free within myself to talk about until my season of affliction where the perfect storm seemed to have gotten the best of me. I hid and almost lost the me, which God had created. It is the testimony of how everything actually can and will change when God becomes the builder. He is the only one who is able to go deep to the core and completely eradicate the residue of your pain but He will not do so until you give him access. So many, instead of confronting their hidden pain go through life victims to themselves. Their hurt is so deep that self worth is lost. It becomes easier to reject the possibility of better when worse is your best friend.

The enemy afflicted you and meant it for evil but God turned it around for your good. I titled this section, God Blocked It as a way of encouraging every reader that God has been there the whole time. Consider this:

- You should not have been born because mom contemplated abortion. God blocked it!
- You should have been dead due to that car accident. God blocked it!
- You were supposed to be a vegetable in the hospital, dependent on machines. God blocked it!
- The knife was meant to kill you. God blocked it!
- The suicide attempt failed. God blocked it!
- The car accident was meant to kill you. God blocked it!
- He raped you and left you for dead. God blocked it!
- She stripped you of all you had, thought she loved you. God blocked it!
- Mom walked out on you, dad left and never came back. God blocked it!
- You were told you wouldn't become anything. God blocked it!
- You were passed up for promotion and now you have your own company. God blocked it!
- The doctors left you for dead. God blocked it!
- That needle was infected with the HIV bacteria. God blocked it!
- Drugs were destroying you. God blocked it!
- You should still be behind bars. God blocked it!
- This list can continue because the reality is God has blocked the evil that was intended towards you. He has been there this whole time, working behind the scenes. He created you to not so you would perish but that you would have

access to an eternal life filled with His joy and His peace. Regardless the pains you have gone through or are going through just remember that God really does have it. Don't stress about the outcome. He's got this!

Did you know that you could actually begin soaring in God even while you are going through your pain? So many put him on hold and take alternate routes until they better. Then they try to give to God what they think he deserves. If God is the builder, he wants the good, the bad and the ugly of you. He wants it all. Trust God enough to continue the journey you started in Him but with a different attitude. As opposed to holding on to the tools, trust him to release and walk when he says walk and stop when he says stop. He will order your step even in your pain. He will guide your thoughts even in the fog. You will become the plane in flight that is not being flown by what the visual eyes can see but the compass of Gods grace.

Finding Your Inner Peace

There are books and studies on how to find your inner peace, this is not that study. Earlier I wrote about Philippians 4:6-9 and that the antidote for anxiety is peace which comes from praying, supplication and giving thanks. I did not adopt any meditation routines, I did not start yoga nor did I sit in a therapist's chair. I speak no ill of therapists; they serve an excellent purpose for those who need them. I am speaking about a formula that the word of God taught me in the midst of my storm. I prayed and cried out to God constantly. In the process of praying and crying out, I learned to say thank you. I found that the more I said thank you the lighter the burden. I mean, I knew that all was not visibly well but it was well with my soul.

In my prayers, I found scriptures that related to where I was. I reminded God of His word. I prayed less about God rescuing me in my current situation and more about him leading me to where he wanted me to be. Do you know how challenging that is? But I tell you, if you try it, you find that the pain begins to lift and joy returns. Your frown becomes a smile. **It leads you to a place where you inner smile becomes your outward reflection.** You might be saying, I don't know how to pray. Well, do you know how to say thank you Jesus? Do you know how to say, I love you Lord? Do you know how to say, Father help me? If you do, and you do, you know how to pray. You begin the process and all of a sudden the Holy Spirit takes over. Your 30 second prayer now becomes 5, 10, 15 minutes and more. When you do that, peace begins to rest on you.

So how do you say thank you? How do you say thank you when your world is falling around. Well, I'm glad you asked. Look at your terrible situation and find one small thing that reflects a ray of hope and say thank you. After you have done that, look for another. The more you do that, you not only find that your prayers have shifted but your level of gratitude has as well. You then realize that what is happening around you has nothing to do with man but rather the plan and will of God for your life.

I know for the one who does not believe this sounds foolish. I tell you this, however, I am where I am because I let go of me and held on to the Lord. I gave him full power to build my house. He is doing it from the inside out and it feels oh so good. I do not need affirmation from man because God has already given His stamp of approval. I am not saying I may not shed more tears. I am not saying the ground beneath me wont crumble again. I am saying that when it happens I know how to find peace in the midst of it all.

Reference

Hamlet by William Shakespeare, between 1599 and 1602

The Diary of the Wolf-Children of Midnapore by The Reverend J.A. L. Singh, 1920

2010 Chilean Earthquake, source Wikipedia, adapted source May 23, 2015

www.ingramcontent.com/pod-product-compliance
Lightning Source LLC
LaVergne TN
LVHW051604070426
835507LV00021B/2766